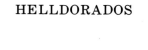

HELLDORADOS

Helldorados, Ghosts and Camps of the Old Southwest

By

NORMAN D. WEIS

PHOTOGRAPHS AND MAPS BY THE AUTHOR

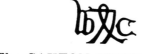

The CAXTON PRINTERS, Ltd.
Caldwell, Idaho 83605
1977

© 1977 by
The CAXTON PRINTERS, Ltd.
Caldwell, Idaho

Library of Congress Cataloging in Publication Data

Weis, Norman D
    Helldorados, ghosts, and camps of the old South-
west.
    Bibliography: p.
    1. Cities and towns, Ruined, extinct, etc. —
Southwestern States. 2. Mines and mining — South-
western States — History. 3. Southwestern States —
History, Local. I. Title.
F786.W37   979   73-83117
ISBN 0-87004-243-2

Lithographed and bound in the United States of America by
The CAXTON PRINTERS, Ltd.
Caldwell, Idaho 83605
122503

In pleasant memory of time shared
with L. L. and N. L. Weis.

CONTENTS

Page

Page

LIST OF ILLUSTRATIONS

Page

Page

Page

PREFACE

TRUTH SPRINGS EASILY from the young and the very old. The old-timer has outlived his inhibitions, and the youngster has yet to feel the need or precaution. Their frank assessments and blunt statements are refreshing in a time when studied obscurity is often the rule.

Old-timers and youngsters have played an important part in this book. Without them much wisdom, humor, and history would be missing. To them I owe my greatest debt.

In the process of visiting, photographing, and gathering information on the several hundred sites from which material for this book was selected, much help was offered by strangers that I now count as friends.

As the text was assembled, valued assistance was rendered by a number of talented individuals.

To the following, I would like to tender my warmest thanks:

Mike Herbison, Head of Libraries, University of Colorado, Colorado Springs, whose objective criticisms have always been valued;

My wife, Jay, who has typed each of these nearly 60,000 words at least four times;

Senator Gale McGee of Wyoming, for assisting in the procurement of maps both current and historical;

Darwin Fetters of Nipton, California, C. F. Thorpe of Cordes Junction, Arizona, and John Strahan of Ouray, Colorado, for taking the time to pour over a multitude of maps;

Grace Middleton of Silver King, Arizona, just for being Grace Middleton;

Slim Riffle of Red Mountain, California, who burned his steak while telling me about old Atolia;

C. O. Carlson and Olive Hunt, who loaded me down with ore samples and fossils;

Yancy Perea and Gene Vick, the twelve-year-old sages from Los Cerrillos;

And my very special thanks to the old-timer from the

Mayer, Arizona, area who insisted that he remain "unanimous." His tales were grand, and with a little scrubbing I was able to include most of them. Assuredly I will honor his request — his identity will always remain "consequential" with me.

INTRODUCTION

IT MAY HAVE BEEN a wild and woolly helldorado, a desolate mining camp high above timberline, or a stubborn community of farmers joined in an improbable endeavor.

Whatever the nature of the town, its reason for existence evaporated. It may have been the collapse of overblown stocks, pinched-out veins, or the realization that the extremes of nature were beyond domestication. In any event, the citizenry vacated — if not entirely, at least to an overwhelming degree.

With the passage of time, the reason for the town's existence and the cause of its demise may have become clouded. The long-deserted remains of once-active towns become a fascinating challenge to anyone possessing a modicum of curiosity.

Some deductions are easy. Square nails gave way to machine-made round nails in 1885, therefore an old hotel with square nails was probably built before 1885. Tin cans with hand-soldered dots centered in the tops were last made in 1915; ergo, a round-nailed shack with solder-dot cans strewn about was built after 1885 and probably deserted prior to 1915.

Generally, local museums and libraries can provide a reasonably complete history of the deserted towns in a given area. However, in the case of the little-known site, little of worth can be found in the existing literature. Occasionally an old-timer can be sought out, but some towns (like Wolf, Colorado) defy complete deduction and permit only a speculative history to be drawn.

Researching the little-known site, however, is easy compared to the original determination of its existence and location. Much of my effort was directed toward that end.

To find an unknown site by direct ground search of an area might take a lifetime. By air the job would be easier but prohibitively expensive. A third method would be to scan a few thousand maps. The last option is at present the only one available to me, although I am working on a means of making economical air search possible.

The United States has carried out a geological survey for nearly one hundred years. Maps of the West have been drawn in great detail and published for general use since 1896. The first places to be mapped were the population centers and the mineralized areas. The latter show a great number of mining towns and camps, most of which were short-lived. Frequently two maps of the same area, but of different dates, will reveal the sudden shrinkage indicative of a newly deserted town. Even with just one map available a number of likely "unknowns" can be pinpointed by scanning carefully for mine shafts, tunnels, dead-end railroads, and unoccupied buildings. Topographic maps that show the ground surface and cultural developement in sufficient detail for such study are available from the United States Department of the Interior, Geological Survey, Denver Federal Center, Denver, Colorado, 80225.

The *Howardsville, Colorado, 7½ minute* topographic map, scaled 1 to 24,000 (that's about three inches to the mile) shows the ground surface in extreme detail. A section of that map is reproduced here.

Howardsville (A), at the upper left corner, shows an aerial tramway connecting an empty rectangle in town with another rectangle half a mile up the hill. The tramway is labeled, "abandoned," which indicates that the mine above and the mill below are probably very old. A trail shown leading to the mine invites on-site inspection. The Pride of the West Mill is shown in black and appears to be operating; however, the map is dated 1955, and the mill may have closed down in the interim.

A search of the literature shows that Howardsville was a rather well known but small ghost town with one mill still operating. Obviously the Pride of the West had not shut down. Howardsville was selected as a site worth visiting, primarily due to the number of old mine camps evident on the map. Any one of them could be a worthwhile, little-known site.

On visitation, the old mill at Howardsville was found to be a marvel worth several rolls of film. The mine and mill complex at (B) and (C) turned out to be a disappointment. The mill was completely gone, and little evidence of the Old Hundred Mine could be discerned with field glasses.

An early summer snow prevented my visiting (E), the

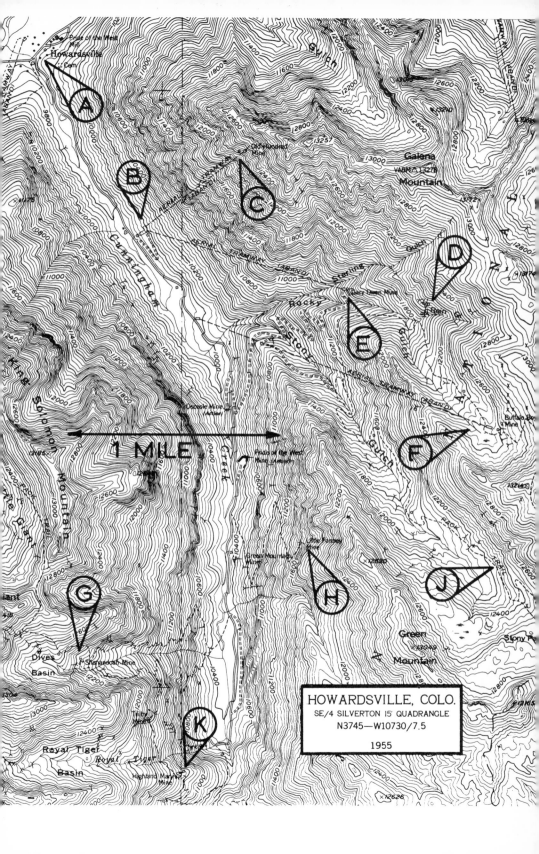

1 MILE

HOWARDSVILLE, COLO.
SE/4 SILVERTON 15' QUADRANGLE
N3745—W10730/7.5

1955

Gary Owen Mine, and (D), the unnamed mine on Rein
Gulch. The four buildings and six tunnels, all in a cluster,
still intrigue me. I will hike up there some summer day,
and while I'm at it I'll visit the Buffalo Mine (F), and
perhaps circle about so as to take the pack trail, (J), back to
the road. The pack trail and the road were part of the
original route into the area. That route came up the head-
waters of the Rio Grande River, then topped over Stony
Pass, on down Stony Gulch, to Howardsville.

The Little Fanney Mine, (H), clings to the hillside, making a great photograph for those owning a long lens. The
Highland Mary Mine, (K), was once a town of the same
name. I had great hopes that this site would hold a number
of buildings but found only foundations. Glassing the hillside showed that item (G), The Shenandoah, was not worth
a 2,000-foot climb. All in all, the area was a bust, except for
Howardsville and the Little Fanney.

My map analysis of the six southwestern states revealed
nearly a thousand possible "unknowns." A search of existing literature showed the great majority to be, in fact,
rather well known. Of the remaining two hundred or so,
less than one in ten proved worthwhile. Many were wiped
out. Others had been reactivated.

The topographic maps most commonly used in this type
of research are the 7½ minute (3 inch to the mile) and the
15 minute (1 inch to the mile). The designation of 7½
minute or 15 minute refers to the angles of latitude and
longitude included on the map. Of course there are 60
minutes to a degree, and 360 degrees make a great circle of
the earth. The important thing to remember is that the 7½
minute map shows only one-fourth the area of a 15 minute
map but shows it in four times the detail.

Although the *Paradise Peak, Nevada, 15 minute* map is
of lesser detail than the Howardsville 7½ minute map, it
contained more in the way of possible "unknown" sites.
The portion of the map reproduced here includes the area
from Gabbs, Nevada, at the southwest, to Lodi Tank at the
northeast.

Items (A) and (B) represent towns supposedly still active
— active as of 1948, the date on the map. The towns, however, might have been deserted in the past 25 years. Item
(C), Downeyville, was listed as a site, meaning it was a
deserted town twenty-five years ago. No buildings are
shown, but more than twenty shafts and numerous prospects are indicated. Items (D), (E), and (F) looked promis-

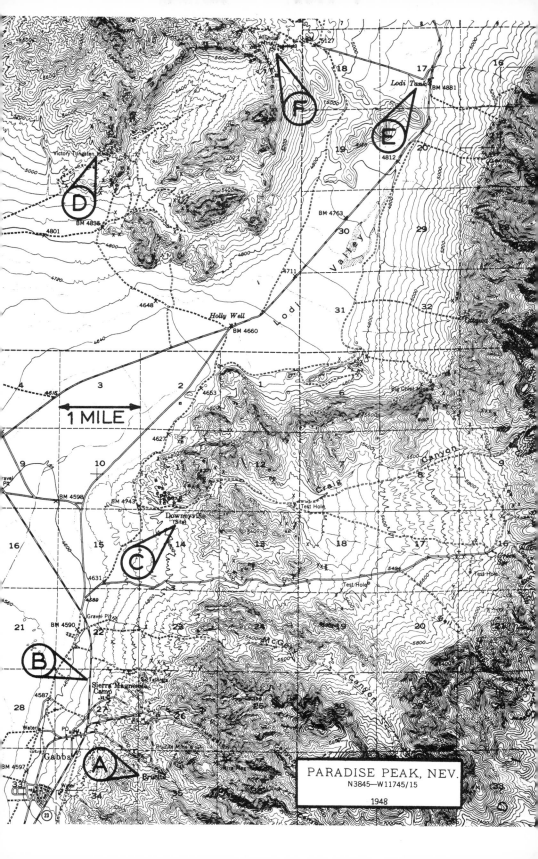

PARADISE PEAK, NEV.

N3845—W11745/15

1948

ing — especially (F), the Illinois Mine Camp. Four empty squares and eight solid squares indicated that the camp consisted of twelve buildings, eight of which were residential in nature. On top of that, the mine was labeled "inactive." It looked like a good prospect, provided it had not been totally destroyed or reactivated since 1948.

When I visited the Gabbs area I found Brucite, (A), to be part of a large, open-pit mine. (B), the Sierra Magnesite Camp, was nothing but concrete slabs. At Downeyville, (C), there was nothing. The Victory Tungsten Mine, (D), was a small mine still operating. Lodi, (E), once quite a town, was now just one small water tank. But (F), The Illinois Mine Camp, was indeed a find.

Only a few of the dozen buildings were standing, but the remains at the site posed an interesting puzzle, ultimately pieced together by a search of the grounds and subsequent visits with informed people at Gabbs. The Nevada State Archives eventually provided a small additional amount of information, mostly about the old town of Lodi. Of the sixteen possible unknowns on the two maps, only one had proved to be virgin of print and worthy of a day's research.

Compared to the difficulties encountered in locating the worthwhile site, recording the remains on film was simple — provided the elements were cooperative. I made it a practice to spend the night in most of the deserted communities, in order to have the advantage of evening and morning light. Bleached boards respond well to black-and-white photography, provided the light plays across the surface to accent the grain and warp of the wood. Sometimes an hour's wait, or a return for a last shot from a particular angle, made an ordinary scene into something spectacular. Staying overnight also permitted experimenting with time exposures by moonlight. Interesting and surprising results can be obtained if time and film are spent freely.

During my 7,000-mile tour of the Southwest, more than 300 rolls of film were exposed, copious notes were taken, and a great number of old-timers, near-old-timers, youngsters, and former residents were interviewed. Most folk were willing to visit; however, some required a bit of cajoling. My interviewing techniques have always been less than spectacular and are often abrupt to the point of alienation. Lately there has been some improvement. My approach has graduated from "foot in mouth" to "tongue in cheek."

Old-timers are often reluctant to talk with a stranger,

TOPOGRAPHIC MAP SYMBOLS

VARIATIONS WILL BE FOUND ON OLDER MAPS

'd surface, heavy duty road, four or more lanes . . . . . .

'd surface, heavy duty road, two or three lanes . . . .

'd surface, medium duty road, four or more lanes . . . .

'd surface, medium duty road, two or three lanes . . . . .

roved light duty road . . . .

mproved dirt road and trail . . . .

al highway, dividing strip 25 feet or less . . . .

al highway, dividing strip exceeding 25 feet . . . .

d under construction . . . .

road, single track and multiple track . . . .

roads in juxtaposition . . . .

row gage, single track and multiple track . . . .

road in street and carline . . . .

ge, road and railroad . . . .

wbridge, road and railroad . . . .

tbridge . . . .

nel, road and railroad . . . .

rpass and underpass . . . .

ortant small masonry or earth dam . . . .

n with lock . . . .

n with road . . . .

al with lock . . . .

dings (dwelling, place of employment, etc.) . . . .

ool, church, and cemetery . . . . Cem

dings (barn, warehouse, etc.) . . . .

er transmission line . . . .

ephone line, pipeline, etc. (labeled as to type) . . . .

ls other than water (labeled as to type) . . . . oOil . . . . . oGas

ks; oil, water, etc. (labeled as to type) . . . . • ● ● ⊘Water

ated or landmark object; windmill . . . . o

n pit, mine, or quarry; prospect . . . . ✕ . . . . ✕

ft and tunnel entrance . . . . Y

Horizontal and vertical control station:

Tablet, spirit level elevation . . . . BM △ 5653

Other recoverable mark, spirit level elevation . . . . △ 5455

Horizontal control station: tablet, vertical angle elevation VABM △ 9519

Any recoverable mark, vertical angle or checked elevation △ 3775

Vertical control station: tablet, spirit level elevation . . . . . BM ✕ 957

Other recoverable mark. spirit level elevation . . . . ✕ 954

cked spot elevation . . . . ✕ 4675

hecked spot elevation and water elevation . . . . ✕ 5657 50

Boundary, national . . . .

State . . . .

County, parish, municipio . . . .

Civil township, precinct, town, barrio . . . .

Incorporated city, village, town, hamlet . . . .

Reservation, national or state . . . .

Small park, cemetery, airport, etc. . . . .

Land grant . . . .

Township or range line, United States land survey . . . . . .

Township or range line, approximate location . . . .

Section line, United States land survey . . . .

Section line, approximate location . . . .

Township line, not United States land survey . . . .

Section line, not United States land survey . . . .

Section corner, found and indicated . . . . + ... +

Boundary monument: land grant and other . . . . □ . . . . □

United States mineral or location monument . . . . ▲

Index contour . . . .   Intermediate contour . .

Supplementary contour . . . .   Depression contours . .

Fill . . . .   Cut . . . .

Levee . . . .   Levee with road . . . . . .

Mine dump . . . .   Wash . . . .

Tailings . . . .   Tailings pond . . . .

Strip mine . . . .   Distorted surface . . . . .

Sand area . . . .   Gravel beach . . . .

Perennial streams . . . .   Intermittent streams . .

Elevated aqueduct . . . .   Aqueduct tunnel . . . . . .

Water well and spring . .   Disappearing stream . .

Small rapids . . . .   Small falls . . . .

Large rapids . . . .   Large falls . . . .

Intermittent lake . . . . .   Dry lake . . . .

Foreshore flat . . . .   Rock or coral reef . . . . .

Sounding, depth curve .   Piling or dolphin . . . . .

Exposed wreck . . . .   Sunken wreck . . . .

Rock, bare or awash; dangerous to navigation . . . . *   ⊛

Marsh (swamp) . . . .   Submerged marsh . . . .

Wooded marsh . . . .   Mangrove . . . .

Woods or brushwood . . .   Orchard . . . .

Vineyard . . . .   Scrub . . . .

Inundation area . . . .   Urban area . . . .

especially one who takes notes. On a number of such occasions I found the application of tongue oil (a cold beer from the cooler) to be of great value. The sociability that resulted generally overcame any suspicions.

Of the more than two hundred sites visited, sixty-seven have been chosen for inclusion in this book. The selection includes wild towns, quiet camps, some well-known ghost towns, and a smattering of "unknowns."

It has been a long but enjoyable endeavor locating and visiting each of these sites. Darkroom work and writing of the text has brought added satisfaction. I wish an equally pleasant experience to all those who tour "Helldorados, Ghosts and Camps of the Old Southwest."

PART I
CALIFORNIA

CALIFORNIA AREA 1

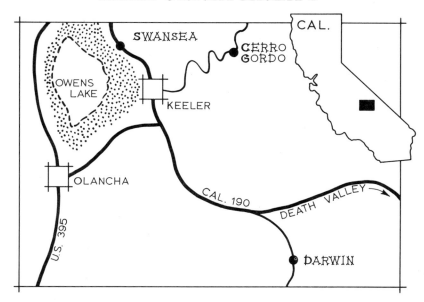

CERRO GORDO, CALIFORNIA

MORTIMER BELSHAW was a shrewd man. Shrewd! Outwardly Belshaw showed only mild interest in the sample of silver-bearing quartz shown around by a Mexican prospector. He inquired of other deposits in the area, and when told that galena was found nearby he immediately laid plans. He knew that the lead found in galena was necessary to subtract silver from its ore. The man who controlled the lead could control the silver, and Belshaw figured to be that man.

Belshaw arrived in Cerro Gordo in 1868. Prospectors were swarming about the rounded, almost fat hills for which the site was named. While the prospectors sought out and claimed the silver, Belshaw quietly sewed up most of the galena deposits. He hastened to spread the word that he planned to build a smelter, then he promptly traded one-fifth of his imaginary smelter for one-third of the Union Mine, the last hold-out containing high-quality galena.

With a few ingots laboriously smelted from his best ore samples, Belshaw headed for San Francisco. Financier Abner B. Elder looked at the ingots, believed Belshaw's

The trackless trestle of the old Union Mine curves
high over the remains of Cerro Gordo.

claims, and promptly offered to back the enterprise. The
Union Mining Company was formed.

By midsummer the partners had constructed a wagon
road from Owen's Lake up the steep slopes to Cerro Gordo.
The road climbed 4,800 feet in its eight serpentine miles. At
one narrow spot a tollgate was installed. Belshaw and
partner didn't plan to miss a trick. The fee was $1.00 per
wagon, two bits per rider. The partners soaked everyone —
and took a double whack at competitors.

Belshaw was a talented engineer, designing and building a smelter capable of turning out four tons of lead-silver
amalgam each day. Charged with coke and coal, and making use of a unique double-boiler principle, it constituted a
major breakthrough in contemporary smelting. One
hundred and twenty bars of lead-silver amalgam were
poured and hauled out each day.

With rear wheels chained and skidding, and front wheel

*Hoops that once held wooden, slatted vats together now
frame the buildings at the upper end of town.*

brakes frequently applied, the eight-mule teams slipped
and slid down the road, traversing dozens of tight switchbacks. The bars were transferred to steamers at the east
bank of Owens Lake, then again loaded on wagons at the
west bank and hauled to San Francisco.

The Union Mining Company built a second smelter in
1890, and production doubled. Traffic increased on the tollroad as other mines expanded production. A new smelter
at Swansea, on the shore of Owens Lake, made lower-grade
ore a paying proposition in spite of Belshaw's tollroad
rates. Belshaw tried to lure business away from the
Swansea Smelter by letting the tollroad go bad. This limited the loads that could be carried in the wagons, and in
effect raised the toll. Competing mines either paid
Belshaw's high smelting fees or forked over a healthy toll.

Belshaw's competitors attempted to build a new road in
to Cerro Gordo, but efforts proved fruitless. The canny

*Massive waste dumps of the Union Mine seem to
threaten the existence of Cerro Gordo.*

Belshaw had placed his tollroad in the only usable spot!
Some disgruntled folk established a tent town below
Belshaw's tollgate and hiked cross-country a mile or so to
Cerro Gordo for supplies and entertainment.

The fifty-six teams of fourteen mules that hauled freight
to Cerro Gordo continued to pay Belshaw's heavy toll.
Later an aerial tramway was built, easing the strangle-
hold of the tollroad. No engine was required to power the
tramway, since its problem was one of slowing the head-
long downhill run of ore-laden buckets. Elaborate braking
mechanisms were utilized, and freight was put in the
buckets on the "up" line when possible.

The town prospered during the seventies, with the population riding between two and three thousand. Several
sporting houses were flourishing. The dance halls of Lola
Travis and Maggie Moore were busy, and the American
Hotel, opened in 1871, continued to do business in spite of
spectacularly high rates. When a young doctor came to
town intending to open a practice, he was confronted with

*The American Hotel, built in 1871, is
the fanciest structure in town.*

One of the smaller sporting houses in town.
Note the tiny rooms or cribs.

drunks, fights, and even gunplay. The doc left town that same evening.

Cerro Gordo enjoys a unique setting. Thirty miles away, to the northwest, 14,495-foot Mount Whitney towers over the dry flats of Owens Lake, besting Cerro Gordo and its adjacent peak by more than a mile. To the east, again thirty miles away, is a "sink" fed infrequently by Salt Creek and the Amargosa River. Better known as Death Valley, its elevation is 282 feet BELOW sea level. Midway between the highest and lowest points in the continguous states, Cerro Gordo enjoys a climate that is the best of the

The Cerro Gordo "Town Council": Jack Smith, Barby Smith (Mayor), Cecil Smith, and a "stranger," Rod Rodriquez.

two extremes. Days are warm and dry — nights pleasantly cool.

Barby and Jack Smith have owned the mine and town since 1949. They charge a dollar to visit the place, and it's well worth it. Their protective presence has prevented the slow, certain destruction suffered by other ghost towns. They have made few changes, except that Jack now claims the town has running water — he runs and gets it twice a week.

Most spectacular in town is the old American Hotel, still replete with square nails, balcony, gazebo, and huge kitchen stove. The trestle of the Union Mine curves over the northern extreme of the business district. A three-crib sporting house still stands next to a string of buildings that once served as stores, warehouses, and machine shops.

Occasional bottle-diggers are permitted limited access. The old mine dump had been used as a garbage dump, with fresh rock tumbled over each day's refuse, creating a gold

Cerro Gordo by moonlight. Owens Dry Lake is in the background.

mine of old bottles inconveniently spread at the extreme bottom of the huge dump.

Fred Kille, teacher and ghost town hunter, has poked and dug around the area extensively. He has located a number of little-known settlements and mines, particularly in the Panamint Valley, next to and parallel to Death Valley. His bottle collection is outstanding. We discussed the hazards involved in digging for bottles and the additional thrills involved in getting to some of the area's ghost towns. He and his wife consider the road to Cerro Gordo "tame and enjoyable." My opinion differed greatly.

The road is narrow and steep — so steep that my (admittedly tired) pickup could make no more than eight miles an hour, floor-boarded. It had not been an enjoyable trip up the hill. The sun was flat in my face on the steep grade a mile below town. The road was but a narrow shelf, and, as I rounded out on top, the sun on the dusty windshield blocked all vision ahead. I locked the transmission, jamed on the brake, and got out to have a look. It was well I did, for the road doubled back to the right. Dead ahead was nothing but space. The only part of the road I enjoyed was the parking place at the end of it.

Going down the hill the next day, I was thinking about the chainlocked wheels on the ore wagons that used to skid around the bends. I forgot about the blue-sky hairpin turn and got the same damned unwanted thrill a second time.

MAP NOTE: Cerro Gordo and a number of small satellite towns and mining camps are shown on the New York Butte, California, 15 minute United States Geological Survey topographic map.

SWANSEA, CALIFORNIA

Trailing broad wakes and spouting dense clouds of smoke, the steamers *Mollie Stevens* and *Bessie Brady* often met in the middle of Owens Lake. Each in turn carried wood on the fourteen-mile journey eastward and silver-lead amalgam on the return. Eighty-five feet long and shallow of draft to suit the meager depths of Owens (salt) Lake, the twin steamers plied between Cartago at the southwest bay and Keeler and Swansea on the northeast shore.

Swansea, named for its larger twin in Wales, was a smelting town. Silver ore from the Inyo Mountains near Cerro Gordo was processed here, with the aid of the local lead and salt deposits. Lead ore in the form of galena came from the Sunset, Union, Morning Star, and Cerro Gordo mines. Unfortunately the salt of Owens Lake was of the carbonate variety, unusable for smelting. The proper chloride salt lay fourteen miles away, over the top of the Inyo Mountains and downhill north to Salt Lake. A tramway carried salt up the 8,000-foot climb through Daisy

Rock building in center is probably part of the old town of Swansea. Much of the original townsite has been covered with shifting sand dunes.

Only a small portion of Swansea's famous smelter is standing.

Canyon from Salt Lake to the mountain pass, then down to a port at the north end of Swansea.

The huge furnaces at Swansea turned out 150 bars of silver every fourteen hours, each weighing a standard eighty-three pounds. It is difficult to imagine the massive operations of smelting and freighting that took place on the shores of Owens Lake. It's especially difficult because Owens Lake is no more.

The same long-term change in climate that created extensive salt flats in the area reduced Owens Lake to a small puddle. Dried up and crusted over, the treacherous lake defies travel over its surface by man or machine. The *Mollie Stevens* and the *Bessie Brady* are out there buried beneath the salt, engines rusted and steam whistles silent.

The smelter chimneys have fallen, and the houses are almost gone — moved or covered with the blowing sand dunes. Only the rock furnaces remain, along with a few buildings of town now owned by the Penn Mines. Four miles away the once-busy port of Keeler escapes complete desertion, thanks to the employment demands of a small soda evaporation plant.

MAP NOTE: Swansea, Keeler, Salt Lake, and the tramway connecting the two can be located on the New York Butte, California, 15 minute United States Geological Survey topographic map.

DARWIN, CALIFORNIA

The story is classic — the party of exhausted men were camped in the Argus Range of California. Water was short, and their food was gone. Their best rifle was found to be short one of its sights, and the chance of shooting game seemed remote. An Indian guide saved the day by repairing the sight with a chunk of soft, white metal. The members of the party knew it was silver and assumed the Indian knew of a considerable deposit — but escape from the hostile area was deemed more important than a search for silver.

Years later Dr. E. Darwin French led a party into the Argus Range to seek out the silver lode. Dr. French, a Ft. Tejon rancher and habitual prospector, had been in the area before — and was likely a member of the starving party that had passed through earlier.

It is not clear whether the Indian's "Gunsight Lode" was ever found, but good signs were evident, and a number of claims were staked. The town that sprang up was officially

Deserted main street of Darwin. Note the anemic D on the hillside.

Defunct post office-general store once sold Green Streak Gasoline.

named Darwin in 1860, long after Dr. E. Darwin French had left to prospect elsewhere.

The Darwin Hills, east of town, eventually yielded more than $3 million worth of silver. Three smelters operated from 1875 to 1880. The town declined, due to depleted ore bodies, in the late eighties and was reduced to one operation by 1913.

The business district is presently deserted. The pumps at the old gas station are broken — even the glass disc at the top is fractured, making it difficult to read the label, "Green Streak Gasoline."

At the old school building a crude plywood sign leans on

*Darwin's little schoolhouse apparently served
other purposes from 1876 to 1900.*

the front, pathetically offering an historic note. Its confusing message indicates it was built in 1876 but not used until 1900, then abandoned in 1917.

To the north of Darwin's business district are the extensive remains of a large company town. The company town has twice as many homes as Darwin, plus a school and hospital. The huge complex has been closed for fifteen years. Row upon row of identical bachelor's cubicles stand unoccupied, with doors open and windows broken. The wind blows clouds of yellow mill tailings over town, heaping obscurity on top of desertion.

MAP NOTE: The Darwin, California, 15 minute United States Geological Survey topograph map shows Darwin and the deserted company town.

Extensive company town just north of Darwin
has been empty for fifteen years.

CALIFORNIA AREA 2

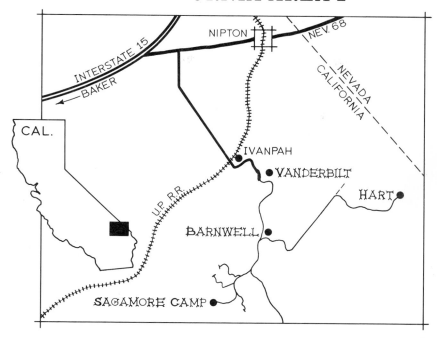

HART, CALIFORNIA

IT IS THE little-known site that attracts the diligent ghost town hunter. The desert west of Needles, California, is full of old camps and deserted towns — an ideal area to explore.

Darwin Fetters of Nipton, California, has poked about the region extensively. He has relied heavily on the available topographic maps but is quick to state that he has visited a number of deserted settlements that are not shown on any of the existing topographic maps. I asked Mr. Fetters about the old towns of Vanderbilt, Hart, Barnwell, Ivanpah Springs, Juan, and Crescent. He had been to all of the sites and recommended Hart and Vanderbilt. In addition he suggested a visit to a little-known mining camp called Sagamore and a mysterious place he called Mescal City.

Thirty-nine miles east of Baker, California, Highway 15-91 makes a broad bend to the north. At this spot a lesser blacktop road heads east and in four miles branches to the south. In three more miles it angles slightly, then heads in a precisely straight line for the deserted railroad town of

Ivanpah. About four miles past Ivanpah the tar becomes gravel, and the Dakar Minerals Development sign can be seen on the left side of the road, near the site of the old town of Vanderbilt.

I was disappointed to learn that the last building in Vanderbilt, an old saloon, had recently collapsed and been cleared away. The lone resident of Vanderbilt, Robert D'Anella, furnished some interesting information about most of the old towns in the area, including a special note on Mescal City, which he explained had recently been reclaimed. D'Anella suggested it would be best if I stayed away from that old camp. "They sometimes shoot at strangers up there — trying to protect a contested claim." With a grin he added, "Course they just shoot to scare you, but then they don't shoot too awful straight either."

I decided to look into the Mescal City situation on my way out of the area and to concentrate in the meantime on Hart, Barnwell and Sagamore Camp.

Four miles south of Vanderbilt the water tower at the site of Barnwell is visible on the left. At this point a gravel road exits to the east. In nine miles the road ends at the foot of Castle Mountain — smack in the middle of the old town of Hart, California.

The flats adjacent to the mountains are strewn with old boards, barrel hoops, wagon wheel rims, broken bottles, and rusted tin cans of the early 1900s. The chimney of the old Norton residence looms at the northwest edge of the townsite. Toward the slopes are remains of a second-effort mining operation involving a white clay or some claylike compound of sodium or potassium. The mineral deposits still on the site are brilliant white and, under a noon sun, irritating to the unprotected eye.

To the south are the remains of several old gold mines. One of the shafts is said to extend 835 feet down. I dropped a stone, and after ten seconds I could still hear it faintly clattering. To the east is what appears at first glance to be an oil well. Noting the height of the storage tank, it becomes obvious that it was at one time the town's water supply. Robert D'Anella of Vanderbilt told me later that the wooden walking beam and accessory equipment were carted in from San Francisco on a set of six-foot wheels. A small engine once turned an eccentric operating the walking beam so as to piston water up from the underground pool hundreds of feet below.

Gold was discovered in the ledges along the slopes of the

Chimney of the old Norton residence in Hart
is framed by branches of a Joshua tree.

Showing signs of two renovations, cabin at east end
of Hart appears to be in need of a third.

Wooden barrel hoops form a figure eight around the old stirring paddle at an unnamed gold mine and mill on the hill above Hart, California.

Strange device was probably used to break clay deposits during second-effort mining in Hart.

The wooden flywheel and walking beam of Hart's municipal water system were carted in from San Francisco in 1900.

mountain in December of 1907. The ore was rich, and promoters and prospectors invaded the territory. Within a month, 300 people were camped on the site, and a newspaper, the *Hart Enterprise*, was selling copies of its first edition. In April a hotel was constructed, and residents of the town were rapidly replacing tent canvas with more substantial material. A post office was finished in May. In December the bubble burst. The town had flourished for exactly one year. When the mines shut down there was little excuse to continue the town's existence. Hart, it seemed, had always been a long way from anywhere, and, without the mines, the distance increased. The post office held out until 1915. Since that time only sporadic mining has been conducted. Most of the effort was aimed at extracting pockets of clay.

The remains of the town are sparse. Rarely can one

After crushing, clay was roasted and pulverized.

remnant be spotted from the site of another. The cemetery is located somewhere in the middle of the remains, but in two hours of searching I was unable to find it. Most likely it was a small cemetery — after all, how many people could have died in a town that itself died one year after it was born?

MAP NOTE: The Ivanpah and the Crescent Peak, California, 15 minute United States Geological Survey topographic maps are both necessary for a proper exploration of the area.

BARNWELL, CALIFORNIA

Barnwell now consists of two buildings, a windmill, a water tower, and extensive foundations. That's quite a comedown for a town that once had a population measured in the thousands. Walking over the site, it is hard to believe such a thriving community could have existed here. Little reliable information is available concerning the town. However, according to Robert D'Anella, owner of a number of claims in the vicinity, Barnwell was once the largest town in the region and served as the trade center for the entire mining district. Its three slaughter houses furnished meat for the dozens of mine camps in the area.

Originally a stage station, the town boomed when the Atchison, Topeka and Sante Fe Railroad built its line on

Venerable old stage station in Barnwell was the first structure built and the last to remain. Building has been modernized and enlarged a number of times.

the old wagon route. The stage station grew from two rooms to a respectable hotel. Later the California and Eastern Railroad passed through Vanderbilt and apparently made connection with the Sante Fe within the town's limits. From Barnwell another spur headed northeast to the mining camp of Juan. The March 31, 1894 issue of the *Mining and Scientific Press* stated, "The Nevada Southern Railroad is in good order, and regular trips are made to Manvel, four miles from Vanderbilt." No mention is made of Barnwell.

Since Barnwell is exactly four miles from Vanderbilt, and no other townsite can be found on the map that fits the description, one must assume that Manvel was another name given the town of Barnwell.

There is considerable confusion in the early literature of the Vanderbilt Mining District. Promoters often exaggerated their holdings while carefully avoiding mention of competing enterprises, and occasionally small communities were misrepresented as bustling cities. Some of the claims made about Barnwell are probably examples of that practice.

Barnwell was, however, a major junction. At least three, and perhaps four, rail lines met there, and wagon roads eminated from town in three directions. It was truly the "Hub of the Vanderbilt Mining District."

Barnwell held that title until the turn of the century, when mines in the area began to fail. The short-haul railroads shut down — only the Santa Fe remained in operation. Homes were moved from town, and fire destroyed much of the business district.

The stage station, the oldest building in town, was spared. It served as a depot for the Santa Fe for a time. When the Santa Fe was relocated to pass through Ivanpah, several miles away, the old stage station was returned to its original pursuit — catering to road traffic. Now, as in the beginning, it stands alone, a monument to mark the site of the town of Barnwell — once the "Hub of the Vanderbilt Mining District.

MAP NOTE: The site of Barnwell is shown on the Crescent Peak, California, 15 minute United States Geological Survey topographic map.

Water tank at Barnwell appears to have been constructed shortly before stage station was deserted.

SAGAMORE MINE CAMP, CALIFORNIA

Darwin Fetters of Nipton had said, "Take a left a strong mile south past Barnwell, then head to the right — I think — then — well — you'll know you're on the right road if you climb up over a saddle and dump into the middle of a canyon."

The map showed no road to fit the description. There was a road turning off south of Barnwell, but it led to Live Oak Canyon. Sagamore Canyon was shown complete with a road along the stream bed, but there was no connection between the two roads — no way to "dump" into the middle of the canyon.

It would be appropropriate here to give detailed instructions on how to locate Sagamore Camp, but the network of little-used roads makes that nearly impossible. It took me several hours to run half a dozen trails to their destinations in order to find the correct one. On the way out I simply headed east, eventually locating the Barnwell road, but again I found some unexpected dead ends. You will know you are on the right road when you drive through a gate and a dry wash, and start a climb up a winding, rocky road with a steep drop-off into another dry wash to your right. The road is steep enough to let a wheel spin occasionally and rough enough to require dodging an unwanted meeting between boulder and differential. This is the road that "dumps" into the canyon.

Once in Sagamore Canyon mine shacks become visible on the left, and an old railroad grade takes off straight ahead. With a jeep you can find your way down to the dry stream bed then drive up the bed a couple of miles to "tin camp." It's another mile up the canyon to "rock camp," and even with a jeep it's best to cover this section on foot.

"Tin camp" is the result of Sagamore's only major rework. Eight or ten men were employed mining the tungsten overlooked in the original extraction of silver. The largest of the several corrugated sheds is still liveable and occasionally used. A paper plate tacked on the wall bears the following message:

> *"Thanks for leaving this cabin in such a goddam mess. O.K. to use for shelter. Thanks for stealing the stove – you can buy an antique exactly like it for $18 in town."*

"Tin camp" at the Sagamore Mine was built during
the later tungsten mining period.

The location of the camp, smack in the bottom of the canyon, is a tribute to the dry climate. In any valley but this one, rain pattering on a tin roof would most likely lull one to sleep. In Sagamore Canyon it is reason to start packing.

On up the canyon, extensive rock structures line the dry creek bed. A chimney on the right stands without benefit of mortar. Above it, serpentine rockworks form the abutments for the old railroad line that stretched several miles from the mine to a point on the canyon rim. I hiked to the mine "by rail," and returned later "by dry-wash road."

The old Sagamore Mine head frame stands astraddle the shaft on a shelf about fifty feet above the canyon floor. A tunnel bores into the shelf from below, meeting the shaft at the first level. Nearby are the ruins of several rock-walled, dirt-roofed structures. Built prior to 1890, they are very likely the first homes built in the canyon. On down the canyon, via the dry-wash road, numerous rock walls stand in line, some more than ten feet high. Rock forms the front

*Sagamore Mine gallows frame stands over
the collapsed remains of its hoist house.*

*Sagamore was remote, and lime was scarce. Chimneys,
walls, and entire buildings were constructed
with a minimum of cementing agent.*

and sides of the buildings, while the canyon wall makes the rear. Missing are the log roofs and any indication of a wooden second story. Either flood or fire, perhaps both, was responsible for the destruction.

Back in Vanderbilt, D'Anella provided some additional information. He had read or heard somewhere that the original camp dated as far back as 1867 and that the camp employed forty or fifty men to mine silver and smaller amounts of lead and copper. The community probably numbered more than one hundred souls.

When the silver ran out, the mine and camp were abandoned. Many years later tungsten deposits were noted in the old mine. By then "rock camp" had deteriorated beyond use, requiring construction of the newer "tin camp."

I mentioned to D'Anella that there was no sign of a mill at Sagamore Camp or at any of the other mines in the vicinity.

"Most of them were blown up — blown up on purpose," he explained. "Every time Hollywood made a Western, it seems they had to have a big explosion, and old mills were big and real cheap. Blew a lot of them up myself, working for the film companies." Just the thought of it brought a smile to his face. "Used to put dynamite under the eaves and in the foundation corners. Then set off the bottoms and a bit later, on a millisecond delay, blow the roof — spectacular as hell!" He explained further. "That's why you seldom find an intact mill, or even one that's leaned over or collapsed. Most of them are scattered in splinters all over the countryside."

As I drove back along the road leading toward the interstate highway, I realized my route would take me past Mescal City, the place reportedly protected by trigger-happy guards. I got out the maps, located the turnoff, and proceeded full of courage, with telephoto lenses installed. After traveling several miles along the winding dirt road, my progress was blocked by a sturdy gate, stoutly chained and padlocked, happily precluding any possibility of a confrontation with those intent upon protecting a contested claim.

MAP NOTE: Sagamore Camp is shown southwest of Barnwell on the Crescent Peak, California, 15 minute United States Geological Survey topographical map.

CALIFORNIA AREA 3

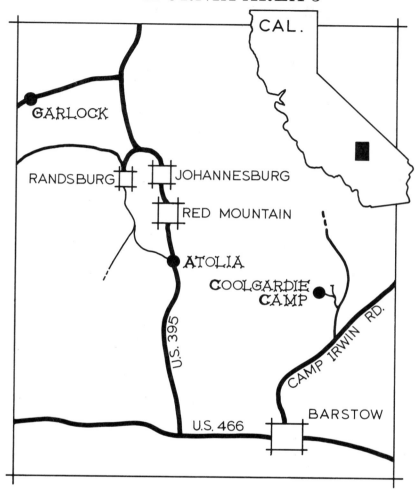

GARLOCK, CALIFORNIA

THE YELLOW ASTER MINE was rich in gold but poor in
water. The mine was awkwardly situated in a deep notch
on the northeast shoulder of Government Peak, one of the
few peaks that make up the Rand Mountains. The highest
peaks are less than 3,000 feet above the desert flats and are
unable to steal moisture from the already dry air. Ore from
the Yellow Aster was hauled to the nearest mill; the mill, of
necessity, was at the nearest water.

Large arrastra was once powered by steam engine. Wooden sprocket pulled four large drag stones in circular manner, crushing gold ore beneath.

Garlock was such a location. Water pumped and piped from a nearby spring was its reason for existence and later the reason for its demise.

Eugene Garlock, in 1896, built a stamp mill here to replace the inadequate capacity of a steam-powered arrastra. Ore was hauled a dozen miles to be crushed, separated by water, and melted into bars. As the mines increased their outputs, so the number of mills increased. With the increased demand and the limited flow from the springs, water became scarce. Wells dug in the area improved the supply, and more mills were built. At its peak Garlock boasted six mills in the immediate area.

The town claimed two hotels, a grocery, two saloons, and several structures that served multiple purposes. Miller's rock structure (still standing) was built in 1897 and served as stage depot, store, and bar.

*Miller Building, erected in 1897, sported a classy, angled
entrance. Building served at various times as
stage station, general store, and bar.*

Fueling the steam engines that supplied power for the
machinery at the mills proved to be a serious problem.
When wood supplies fell short, brush was forked into the
furnaces. Huge quantities were required, and, as a result,
the surrounding area became thoroughly stripped or vege-
tation.

When the Yellow Aster Mine Company built its own mill
a few miles east of Garlock in Goler Gulch, part of Garlock
moved to Goler Gulch. Later it proved more efficient to
pump the water by means of Achimede's Screw through
pipes to the site of the mine proper, six miles to the southeast.

In 1898 a spur of the Atchison, Topeka and Santa Fe
reached the mines on Rand Mountain, and most of the ore
was then shipped to Barstow for more efficient extraction.
Most of the remaining residents of Garlock moved to

*Buildings in Garlock were made of a variety of materials. The two in
foreground are of sawn logs, the one at the rear is adobe.*

Randsburg and Johannesburg, and by 1902 only two
families remained in Garlock.

In 1911 the Southern Pacific built its tracks through
Garlock, and the town was given another breath of life.
Later, salt mining was undertaken on nearby Koehn Dry
Lake. A few families moved in and the post office was
reopened, but in 1926 Garlock re-expired when the post
office closed for the last time.

MAP NOTE: Details of the area, showing a great number of jeep trails,
can be found on the Garlock, California, 7½ minute United States Geological topographic map. More of the older sites are named on the 1943
Saltdale and Randsburg, California, 15 minute maps.

ATOLIA, CALIFORNIA

Atkins and DeGolia, two officers of the Tungsten Mining Company, each offered a part of his name, and the combination came out "Atolia." Some claim that DeGolia only donated the "lia" and that a third man, Pete Osdick, furnished the "o."

The town grew around a number of tungsten mines and reached its peak population in 1914 and 1915. Residences

Tungsten ore was hoisted up the slanted track and dumped into waiting ore cars. Huge quantities of scheelite, an ore of tungsten, were removed from the ground below Atolia.

All of Atolia's many old mines seem to enter the ground at the same peculiar angle. Shafts probably paralleled the slanting beds of ore.

were widely scattered, the flat, rolling land providing an unusual roominess for a mining town.

C. H. (Slim) Riffle, of Red Mountain, just to the north, spent most of his life in the mines of Atolia. There is a modern plant to the south of Atolia, and a few folk live nearby. Slim draws an imaginary line near the plant and calls the numerous deserted mines, houses, and ruins to the north "Old Atolia." Most of the buildings are ramshackle and the mines long deserted — wood bleaching in the sun, ore cars rusting on the dumps. Many of the old mines utilized slanted shafts about twenty degrees off vertical, permitting the skip to skid up and down on wooden rails.

Several large buildings in old Atolia are beginning to show the effects of weather and depredation. Buildings were probably boardinghouses and offices.

"It's always been the tungsten we were after, " says Slim. "In fact, we used to use chunks of the ore — scheelite — for poker chips. That was down at the Tim O'Connor's saloon. Just a tent, really, but he called it the Bucket of Blood."

Slim didn't elaborate, but high-grading must have been a way of life. It was a simple matter to slip some of the better samples in lunch pail or pocket. It wasn't considered exactly legal, but then the mine owners expected it and ignored the loss as long as it was minor. The practice was an early type of fringe benefit. The Union No. 1 Mine west of the old town was the best hole and no doubt offered the best opportunity to pocket an evening's supply of poker chips.

Outside of the usual hotel, livery, pool hall, and saloon, Atolia had a picture show and a dairy. The town hit its first boom in 1914 during World War I, and the population reached several thousand. Shortly after the war, Charlie Taylor and Charlie Churchill, owners of some of the best holdings, sensed an impending bust. They sold out, and within a few years the bottom fell out of the price of tungsten. The population of the town, already depleted, shrunk to a stubborn few.

The area abounds in back roads and old ruins. Nearby Red Mountain, Johannesburg, and Randsburg, all old mining towns, are well worth a visit. A back road connecting Randsburg and Atolia makes a circle tour possible.

MAP NOTE: The 1911 Randsburg, California, 15 minute United States Geological Survey topographic map shows some of the back roads and many of the old mines.

COOLGARDIE CAMP, CALIFORNIA

Eight miles north of Barstow on the Camp Irwin Highway, a graveled route called the Copper City Road exits to the north. Exactly six and a half miles along this road and just over a low pass, a nondescript dirt road heads to the northwest. At this point a multiplicity of interlacing back roads and dune-buggy trails makes eyeball navigation a must. Coolgardie Camp is exactly four miles northwest of the junction and in line with a prominent, but unnamed, knob that rises 800 feet above the flats of Coolgardie Camp.

The remains of the old placer camp are sparse, but the scenery is great. The Joshua trees are magnificent, many

Deserted placer camp of Coolgardie once had
every convenience, even a tree house.

of them growing taller and broader of trunk than the re-
vered specimens in the Joshua National Forest.

Space is plentiful, water is scarce. If you wish to pan out
some sand, be sure to include extra supplies of water.
There are several active claims in Coolgardie Camp, sug-
gesting that care be taken in the choice of panning sites
lest one be guilty of accidental claim jumping.

Dozens of old, deserted mines are to be found in the area,
and a number of geologic features carry names that invite
inspection. There are Opal Mountain, Inscription Canyon,
Superior Lake, Rainbow Basin, and Fossil Canyon. The old
town of Goldstone to the northwest has a wall or two still
standing, and to the southeast is the site of Bismark. Near
Bismark is the restored "ghost town" of Calico — possibly
worth a visit — if you like crowds and enjoy a carnival
atmosphere.

MAP NOTE: The Opal Mountain, Lane Mountain, Barstow, and Daggett,
California, 15 minute United States Geological Survey topographic maps
are all required to tour the area.

CALIFORNIA AREA 4

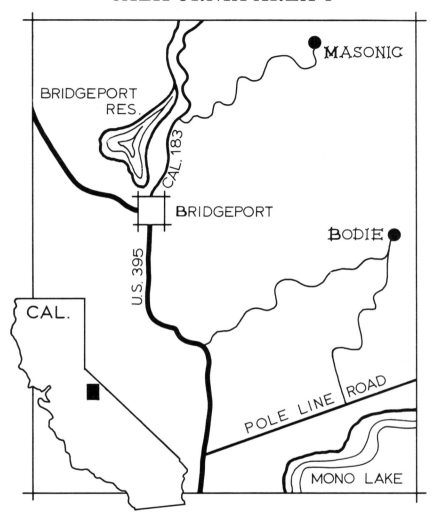

MASONIC, CALIFORNIA

TRACES OF GOLD were found in the narrow, unnamed gulch in 1860. Although rich deposits were present just below the surface, it wasn't until 1900 that Joe Green scratched away the overburden to bring the yellow color to light. The vein revealed was rich, and Joe promptly laid out his claim. Appropriately, he registered the find as the Jump Joe Mine. Two years later Phillips, Bryan, and Dorsey located

Marvelous example of a rock dugout stands at the site of Lower Masonic.

Middle Masonic, once the bustling commercial center of the trio of towns,
now consists of two cabins and numerous piles of rubble.

The Pittsburg Liberty Mill processed ores from its own shaft and from the Serita, half a mile up the hill to the left of photo. Aerial tramway once connected the Serita with the mill.

a richer vein nearby which became known as the Pittsburg Liberty.

By 1907 a sizable camp filled the gulch, separating naturally into three sections — upper, middle, and lower, where the ten-stamp Liberty Mill was sited. Although the population of all three added up to no more than 500, a great many of the 500 were Masons, and it wasn't long before a hall was built. Soon another was constructed and the town named Masonic.

In 1910, after three good years and $600,000 in bullion extracted, the Pittsburg Liberty Company went broke. The body of Phillips, one of the owners, was found at the bottom of the Liberty shaft. Some claimed suicide, others murder, but the records called it an accident.

A second attempt to mine the gulch was made between 1933 and 1938. By that time the town had become nearly deserted, and the new mining did little to attract new citizens.

Masonic has been vacant for more than twenty years. A few shacks and a log building mark the site of Middle

The Chemung Mine, two miles southwest of Masonic,
is in the process of being reactivated.

Remnants of Upper Masonic string out along a
side canyon just east of Masonic Springs.

Collapsed roof of old log cabin gives a rakish appearance to the eaves.

Sunset at the Success Mine on the road between Masonic and Bridgeport.

Masonic. More shacks, mill ruins, and a rock-walled soddy are all that is left of Lower Town. Even the overhead tramway cables have fallen. Upper Town holds a pitiful remnant of collapsed shacks and stubborn log corners.

Not a trace remains of the Masonic Halls, but, according to the map, the name Masonic has survived. It is found on every geologic feature of note within five miles of town. There is Masonic Gulch, Masonic Mountain, Masonic Spring, and Masonic Creek — but there is not a single Mason left in Masonic Town.

MAP NOTE: The Bridgeport, California, 15 minute United States Geological Survey topographic map shows the three sites.

BODIE, CALIFORNIA

History at best is inexact. Four authorities give four different versions of the naming of Bodie Town. Variously, the first man to find gold in the area was named William Bodey, William S. Body, Waterman S. Body, and Waterman S. Bodye. There seemed to be a tie between William and Waterman — and complete confusion concerning the last name. Town fathers decided to name the place Bodie, a spelling known to be wrong but guaranteed to at least achieve proper pronunciation.

The man with the questionable name discovered placer gold at the head of Cottonwood Canyon in 1859. He took his small poke to Monoville and traded it for a winter's worth of food. He and a friend, E. S. Taylor, set out for Bodie, but a blizzard caught them on the way. Taylor wrapped the exhausted Bodie in blankets and went for help. On return he could not find his friend. In fact, Bodie's body was not found until the following spring.

Weather in Bodie was not just a topic of conversation, it

Honeycombed Bodie Bluff overlooks the Standard Mine and the eastern portion of Bodie, California.

One of many windlass-equipped dug wells in Bodie.

View looking east down Green Street. Methodist Church is at left, livery on right.

From left to right, the post office, Odd Fellows Hall, Miners' Union Hall, morgue, and the Boone Store and Warehouse.

Ordinary table saw at left and an early version of a radial-arm saw at the front of the shed. Long support arm pivoted at top, permitting saw to be drawn forward to cut lumber to length.

This old dump wagon is worth an hour of study. Hand-cranked worm gear permitted bottom trapdoors to be closed. A trainlike coupling was installed at each end, permitting reversal without turnabout. Either axle could be locked while remaining axle was used for steering.

was a matter of survival. Many citizens died in the winter of 1878 when twenty-foot drifts were common and wood was in short supply. The 8,600-foot altitude, although it promised mild summers, guaranteed severe winters.

Death by man-made violence was also common — more common than the church-going faction would desire or the Chamber of Commerce would admit. In one week six men were shot to death. The "Bodie 601" vigilance group attempted to control the violence by adding lynching as an alternate to murder.

*Close-up of the 1860 version of the radial-arm saw shows blade,
draw handle, lower drive wheel, and broken drive belt.*

The big boom came to Bodie in 1878 when the Standard
Mine (formerly the Bunker Hill) hit a heavy gold vein. An
earlier discovery of gold in a collapsed working was
eclipsed by the richness of the new find, which ran to $4,000
per ton.

The rush was on, and the population zoomed from several hundred to 10,000 or more. There were eight news-

Hoist works of the Red Cloud Mine, one mile south of Bodie, are now mounted at the western outskirts of town. The peculiar "ribbon" cable measures 1½ by 5 inches in cross section.

papers, and five of them were published daily! A 32-mile railroad was built in 1881, connecting the forested area of Mono Lake with the wood-poor mining town. Quickly Bodie changed from a tent-and-shack community to a wood-and-brick city. And just as quickly, the boom subsided. As the veins thinned, so did the population, and by 1882 there were fewer than 500 folk rattling about a town built for twenty times their number.

But in its short heyday Bodie was a genuine heller. Stages were robbed of bullion so often that the Wells Fargo Company called in their best shots to ride guard on the money runs. Sixty-five saloons, gin mills, and ale stoops were in operation — all of them making money. The Parole Saloon and the Sawdust Corner sought out the ordinary customer, while the Senate and Cabinet lured the carriage trade. Three breweries supplied the draft, and a handful of churches valiantly fought the flow. It was a losing battle, and the cry "Goodby, God, I'm going to Bodie" became common.

Fancy stone marks the grave of Evelyn Myers,
who died just before her third birthday.

*Expansive boardwalks fronted the buildings
on the west side of Main Street.*

Polite folk referred to the sinful part of town as the "red-light district," but, for the customers, Maiden Lane and Virgin Alley held more than red lights. Nellie Monroe, Rosa May, "Beautiful Doll," and Eleanor Dumont, otherwise called "Madam Mustache," ran houses as respectable as any establishments in the state.

When a hydroelectric power plant of thirteen horsepower sent electricty on a thirteen-mile journey to Bodie, the lines were laid out straight for fear the mysterious juice could not navigate sharp corners. It worked! When the switch was closed, a motor in Bodie delivered power, satisfactorily operating the hoist of the Standard Mine. The engineers of the system were quickly sought out to build similar installations throughout the world. It is not know whether they ever ventured to curve their lines.

The James S. Cain Company owned the Midnight Mine adjacent to the Standard Mine. In 1915 the Standard Mining Company was found guilty of tapping the Midnight's vein. As settlement, the Cain Company was given title to the Standard. It was a hollow victory, for there was little gold left in either mine. The railroad gave up service the next year, and only the diehards remained in town.

In 1962 the State of California designated Brodie as a state park, and the considerable remains have been held in a state of "arrested decay." The result is marvelous. No rebuilding is allowed. Looting is prevented. The town remains as it was when deserted. There are no shops, and there is no carnival atmosphere. Occasionally a wedding is held at the old Methodist Church. Even then the spirit of Bodie is honored, as the participants wear costumes of Bodie's boomtown era.

MAP NOTE: The Bodie, California, 15 minute United States Geological Survey topographic map shows the area in detail.

CALIFORNIA AREA 5

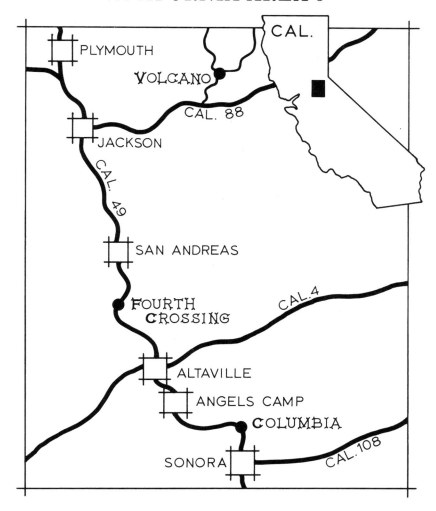

COLUMBIA, CALIFORNIA

AFTER A VISIT TO BODIE it is most appropriate to have a look at Columbia — a living, operating, faithfully restored city of the late 1800s. In 1945 the state legislature voted to preserve Columbia as an historic state park. Careful restoration has been carried out continuously since that time. Here, instead of peeking in the window you can walk in the stores, study the fixtures and the stock, and sometimes purchase period items from approprately attired clerks.

*View to the north along Main Street, with Wells Fargo
building at left, Douglass Saloon in the background.*

Columbia, "The Gem of the Southern Mines," has had a
colorful history. The reporting of its history has been just
as colorful, with exaggerations and embellishments causing a multiplicity of figures and great variation in "fact."

Gold was discovered here by Mexicans in the 1840s — or
by Doctor Hildreth's party in 1850. Believing sudden

*The corner of Fulton and Washington streets in Columbia, California.
Hydraulicked area begins just beyond street end.*

riches might be difficult for foreigners to handle, the Hildreth Party chased off the Mexicans (some deny the Mexicans were there first) and took over the diggings. The place was called Hildreth's Diggings. Later, since only "men of the dominant nationality" were allowed, it was called American Camp.

Within a month 5,000 (some claim up to 8,000) prospectors were panning in the area. The magnitude of the camp suggested a name to match. Columbia was selected, and the camp became a town.

To alleviate the short supply of water, extensive flumes and reservoirs were constructed. The price of sluice water, as charged by the Tuolumne County Water Company, was so high that within a few years the miners formed their own company and began construction of a sixty-mile aqueduct.

By 1852 city streets had been laid out, and 150 (or was it 180?) businesses were in operation. By 1853 Columbia was the third largest city in California, with a population of 10,000 (or 15,000). That year a petition was circulated asking the governor to designate Columbia as the state capitol. The petition, with 10,000 signatures, was stored in

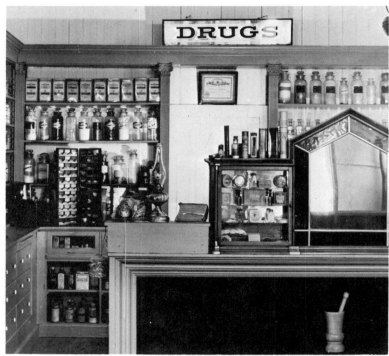

Interior of drugstore on the north side of Columbia's State Street.

the bank, but Senator Coffroth, who was representing a convicted murderer awaiting execution, stole the petition and rewrote the first page to read like a pardon for his client. The man was pardoned, and talk of a state capitol waned.

The city grew, and in 1854 there were 30 (40) saloons, 1 brewery, 1 (2) churches, 143 (160) gambling joints, 17 (23) stores, 4 (8) hotels, 7 bakeries, 4 (8) banks, and 2 (3) theaters. Fire destroyed much of the business district in 1854, and it was rebuilt with brick. The miners' aqueduct was partly built, and Columbia's future looked bright.

Throughout Columbia's history a number of bizarre incidents transpired. The Barclay lynching was perhaps the wildest. Here again the variations are many. The second most likely version will again be included in parenthesis.

A fellow named Smith, well under the influence, became annoyed with barmaid Martha Barclay's foul language

Two rock vaults occupy rear portion of the Wells Fargo Depot and Stage Station.

and her demands that Smith vacate the premises. Smith reportedly pushed (slapped) barmaid Barclay just as her husband, John, entered. John shot Smith dead on the spot. A friend of Smith's proceeded to lobby against John's longevity and managed to work up a drunken lynching committee. Once decided, even the sheriff couldn't stop the gang. Barclay was strung up, using a sluice as gallows. The drunken mob had forgotten to tie Barclay's hands, and Barclay was hanging onto the rope for dear life. The miners climbed up on the sluice and jerked the rope (hung onto Barclay's legs), but Barclay's grip was solid. They dropped him repeatedly (or they hoisted a miner atop the sluice to beat Barclay's fists with a pistol butt) until he lost both his grip and his life.

Fire ravaged the central part of town for the second time in 1857. As a result, streets were widened and brick buildings were equipped with fire-and burglarproof steel shut-

*The Eagle Cottage, the Gazette office, and the Fallon Hotel
and Theater line the west side of Washington Street.*

Originally built for the King of Hawaii, fire wagon was found unclaimed in a San Francisco warehouse. Named Papeete, it became Columbia's pride and joy in 1859.

ters. The rebuilding took place in spite of the thinning gold deposits.

The hard-rock and placer mines were subject to great promotions and repeated sales. Salting was a way of life and was carried out in a number of devious ways. Early crude attempts (like shotgunning a load of gold into the tunnel wall) yielded gold on the surface and none beneath. Only a beginner would buy that — and many did.

Salting had been a sophisticated art in the Columbia area since 1851. The art may have reached its zenith when two knowledgeable Chinese, wise to every salting method, looked into the purchase of a placer claim owned by a couple of unprincipled white men. The Chinese were on the lookout for pipe smokers, knowing that gold was often put in with the tobacco and the pipes knocked out innocently in the sluice. They knew about gold-laden sweatbands wiped out while held over the gold pan. In fact, they were ready to resist any destraction that might permit the sly addition of gold and the consequent raise in the asking price of the claim.

The Chinese selected the spot to dig and used their own shovel. The sellers were kept at a distance. When the sluice was half filled, a rattlesnake fell off a nearby hummock, right onto the spot where the Chinese were digging. Quickly one of the sellers fired his shotgun, killing the snake and saving the lives of one or more Chinamen. After profuse thanks were given, the Chinese continued digging, filled the sluice, and washed it through. A surprising amount of dust was found in the riffles, and the claim sold for a fancy price. The old shotgun trick had worked again. The "live" snake had been dead, but the gun shot was real — except the lead had been exchanged for gold dust! Brete Harte put it well when he wrote:

> "The ways of a man with a maid may be strange,
>   yet simple and tame
> To the ways of a man with a mine when buying or
>   selling the same."

The gold just plain ran out in the late fifties. No amount of salting or promoting could save the town. Columbia declined rapidly in 1860. Most of the population reduction occurred that one year as thousands deserted the town. A number of buildings were razed and the ground beneath hydraulicked for gold, right down to bedrock.

The great majority of the old buildings of Columbia have survived. Every year another building is restored to permit full operation. Slowly Columbia is again becoming the "Gem of the Southern Mines."

MAP NOTE: The Columbia, California, 7½ minute United States Geological Survey topographic map shows the area in great detail. The 15 minute map of the same area shows less detail but more of the surrounding area.

FOURTH CROSSING, CALIFORNIA

Three accounts place Fourth Crossing in three different places. Even the plaque at the site mentions a location other than the one occupied. Apparently the original Fourth Crossing was on the South Fork of the Calaveras River, two miles west of the present site. It was probably moved shortly after its establishment to an easier crossing of San Antonio Creek. In spite of the relocation, it remained the fourth crossing on the Stockton-Murphys Stage Road.

Grace Bonte has lived in the old stage depot, now a sheep ranch headquarters, since 1926. She states that the town once boasted nearly two hundred inhabitants, centered about a hotel-saloon-stage station combination, and an

The narrow bridge over San Antonio Creek at Fourth Crossing now caters to travelers on foot and hoof. Old livery is in background; to the right; original stage station is nearly hidden in heavy growth.

Flock of sheep enjoy the shade at high noon
at Fourth Crossing.

expansive livery. A general store, school, and residences probably made up the balance of the community.

Originally Fourth Crossing was a mining town, both placer and hard-rock. The Thorp and North Shaft were the best producers. Later the town became an important stage and freight depot, serving the southern mines of California's mother lode. The narrow, one-way bridge handled traffic adequately until the turn of the century, by which time the mining effort had declined.

Now the old hotel-stage station is overgrown with trees, and the bridge, lined on both sides with woven-wire fencing, is reserved exclusively for sheep and foot traffic. Across the creek, and on the opposite side of the road, are a few deserted buildings of the post-1900 era. One, an old-

Livery at Fourth Crossing.

style gas station, would indicate that the one-way bridge was used for auto traffic before being replaced with a wider bridge a short distance upstream.

MAP NOTE: Fourth Crossing is centrally located on the San Andreas, California, 15 minute United States Geological Survey topographic map.

VOLCANO, CALIFORNIA

The cannon was loaded, primed, and aimed level down the main street of Volcano. The Confederate sympathizers suddenly halted their march on the Union Forces. A flanking move was tried, but the Blues quickly swung the muzzle of Old Abe to bear on the Grey leader. The assault died. Volcano remained a Union town.

It is well that Old Abe was not used, for the "cannoneer" had overloaded the weapon, and if fired it would have

St. George Hotel, built in 1867, graces the lower end of Volcano's Main Street.

Looking north along shaded Main Street toward the old Chinese store. Note the broad rock walk.

blown up, doing more damage to its handlers than to the target.

It all began when Confederate sympathizers secretly organized a branch of the "Knights of the Golden Circle." Discovery of the existence of the pro-Southern group led to the formation of the "Volcano Blues." The Blues, forty-one strong, were equipped with uniforms and small arms.

An undercover agent was planted in the Knights, and it was learned an attempt would be made to take over the town and divert the gold to the Southern cause. To gain the needed edge in firepower, an old ship's cannon was purchased by the Blues and hauled in secretly from San Francisco. The cannon was hidden in a remote shop while a carriage was built for it. Rounded rocks were used in place of ball and grape shot. It was fired only once, and that time for effect only — just to keep the Knights in line.

Volcano is one of California's oldest mining towns. Its boom population of 5,000 dwindled into a handful at one time. Now it numbers almost a hundred. The flavor of the old town has been maintained. There are no neon signs or gas stations in, or even near, the town. Many of the buildings are more than 120 years old.

Gold was found in this craterlike but nonvolcanic area in the summer of 1848. Members of the New York Seventh Regiment Mexican War Volunteers (whose presence in the area has never been satisfactorily explained) were the first to find placer gold in the streams. The winter of '45 was severe, and in the spring two Mexicans happened upon the diggings and found the bodies of two soldiers. Word of the strike spread, and soon the valley, inevitably called Soldiers' Gulch, was swarming with prospectors.

The town grew quickly, as ordinary placer techniques were replaced with large-scale hydraulic operations. Eventually, $90 million worth of gold was to be extracted. By 1858 the town had five churches, a school, various social clubs, three butcher shops, a theater, three breweries, and

Old Abe, the cannon that won the war in Volcano.

Old hydraulic gun, or mammoth, stands at the main intersection in Volcano. Water entered at right, exited at high speed from nozzle at left. Wooden box held rock counterweights.

The first two occupants of Volcano's jail were its builders. Hasp was well removed from door crack to prevent easy picking.

a dozen times that number of saloons. The town had the first library and the first astronomical observatory in California.

After the Civil War production of gold slacked, and in 1868 a number of very well-insured buildings burned to the ground. The old Sibley Brewery, built in 1858, is the only brewery surviving. The jail stands unused at the north end of town, its double-walled two-by-twelves sandwiching sheets of boiler plate. It is claimed that the two men who built it got drunk on their pay and ended up as the jail's first occupants. Across the street, the old Chinese store is in operation as the Trading Post. Beside it, locked securely in its tailor-made enclosure, Old Abe points its muzzle down main street, re-enacting the day it won the war in Volcano.

MAP NOTE: The Mokelumne Hill, California, 15 minute United States Geological Survey topographic map shows Volcano and many other historic sites.

FRENCH CORRAL, CALIFORNIA

Elton O. Smith, born in 1901, has lived in French Corral all his life. His grandparents are buried in the cemetery west of town. He attended grammar school and high school in the school-community center, remodeled from one of French Corral's boom-time hotels of the 1850s. There were four youngsters in his graduating class.

We stood in front of the old school enjoying the late afternoon sun, visiting about the town as Elton knew it.

"That screened-in building in front of the school? That's the old well. Water's down just twelve feet — 'course it goes way on down. There are benches in there — screens keep out the bugs — 'course it's leaning now. Someone ran into it with their car."

Elton was the janitor at the school for a time, receiving $27.00 per year for his morning fire-building and evening sweepup.

"We had a fancy bell up in that tower at one time," he pointed to the vacant tower. "Had three hundred dollars

Elton O. Smith stands in front of the school he once attended and later worked as custodian. Gazebo at right is built around French Corral's community well.

worth of silver in it — before they poured, they melted silver dollars right in it! Someone stole it. The bell broke loose, and they dropped it on the roof — knocked a big hole in it. Sheriff got it back. Supposed to be locked up in the old Wells Fargo building now."

Concerning the boom years in French Corral, Elton Smith related some stories passed on to him by his parents.

"There were 3,800 people here in the fifties. Lots of hydraulic work going on. It was a wild place. Men worked six days then went wild on Sundays. Lots of drinking — some men crawled home on their hands and knees." Elton pivoted to look toward the center of town. "On the Fourth of July one year they dug a cannon in, set it right in the center of town, and a man named Bradford loaded it up. Everyone moved back, and Bradford set it off. He had overloaded it, and it blew his head off — rolled forty feet away, the head that is! He's buried in the cemetery, head

Wells Fargo Office in French Corral is shut tight with fireproof metal doors.

Office of the first long-distance telephone line in the Mother Lode. Built in 1853, line connected the headquarters of the Milton Mining and Water Company in French Corral with French Lake, fifty-eight miles away.

and all." I was tempted to ask if Bradford had moved in from Volcano.

The town started in 1849, when a French settler built a corral to hold his mules. When placer gold was found in the San Juan Ridge, a town grew around the corral. Giant hydraulic guns tore the gold out of the surrounding hillsides. The Raker Act of 1888, one of this country's first environmental laws, brought hydraulic operations to a halt. French Corral faded rapidly. Now less than forty people reside in the area.

The map of Area 5 does not extend north far enough to include French Corral. In lieu of a map, one can drive west of Grass Valley, through Rough and Ready to Casey Corner. Two miles west of Casey Corner, the Bridgeport road exits to the right. About seven miles to the north the road crosses the South Fork of the Yuba River at the site of

Covered bridge south of Camptonville, built in 1860, is still in use.

The longest single-span wooden bridge in the world spans the South Fork of the Yuba River, two miles southwest of French Corral.

*Built by David Isaac Johnwood in 1862, the all-wood bridge
has an unsupported free span of 230 feet.*

the old town of Bridgeport, where an astounding wooden
covered bridge still spans the river. French Corral is three
miles beyond the bridge to the northeast.

The present Bridgeport road was originally called the
Virginia Turnpike, a tollroad servicing the northern extreme of the mother lode. The bridge across the Yuba was
an important part of that tollroad and remains as an example of the excellent workmanship of the era.

Built entirely of wood, except for nails and bolts, the
bridge clears the river in one clean, unsupported, 230-foot
span. It is the longest single-span wooden bridge in the
world, and it is a covered bridge to boot. Built by David
Isaac Johnwood in 1862, with wood cut in his own sawmill,
the bridge served for thirty-nine years as a toll crossing,
then for another seventy years as a public convenience. In
1971 it was closed to heavy traffic. A new highway bridge
was built a short distance upstream. Recently the massive
wooden bridge was declared a California Historical Landmark, and the American Society of Civil Engineering declared it a National Historic Civil Engineering landmark.
It is truly an amazing structure.

A dozen miles to the northeast, near Camptonville,
another wooden bridge spans the lesser width of Oregon

Moonlight over the old schoolhouse of French Corral.
Bell was stolen by vandals, later recovered.

Creek. This bridge, built in 1860, has developed a mild swayback but is still rated safe for 17,000-pound loads. The bridge was floated off its foundations when English Dam broke in 1883. It was pulled back in place, wrong end to, by ox teams.

California has much to offer in the way of historic sights. It abounds in ghost towns of all varieties. Its covered bridges are an unexpected bonus.

MAP NOTE: The Grass Valley and Nevada City, California, 15 minute topographic maps show the area in excellent detail.

PART II
ARIZONA

ARIZONA AREA I

SILVER KING, ARIZONA

GRACE MIDDLETON is an uncommon woman. She is young in heart, old in wisdom, and sassy enough to tell you that her exact age is none of your business! Wrinkles have locked her face in pleasant expression, and her eyes hold an unfailing sparkle. She is willing to visit with an occasional tourist but quick to turn away anyone she suspects of souvenir hunting. She is the owner, manager, and sole resident of Silver King.

Grace and her husband, Gordon, came west to Silver King in 1949. They were seeking solitude and the opportu-

Grace Middleton, Queen of the Silver King.

nity to mine enough silver to maintain their chosen way of
life. Gordon, a mining engineer, had figured the mine dump
could be reworked. New extraction methods would make
the low-grade reject ore a paying proposition. A small
house was constructed, using lumber from the old mine
buildings, and sorting of the dump ore with a bulldozer was
undertaken. Grace became adept with the dozer and on
occasion undertook some blasting on nearby claims.

When her husband died, Grace decided to remain at
Silver King. She may well own the distinction of having
lived in the town longer than any other resident, even
though she arrived there 75 years after the initial discovery. Her life is rugged — and she prefers it that way. She
has no running water, gas, or electricity. A friend stops by
periodically to take her to town to shop and replenish the
water supply. She is content with her life. That content-
ment shows in her face, belying an age of fourscore and
more. She possesses a great sense of history concerning
her town and has indeed been an integral part of that
history for the past quarter century.

In 1872 the army undertook to build a road through Pinal
Range. One of the steep portions of the road became known
as Stoneman's Grade, named after the general in com-
mand. Two soldiers, enlistments expired and happy to be
free of the road crew, headed for the town of Florence.
Near the foot of Stoneman's Grade they noticed a peculiar
outcrop of rock. One of them, named Sullivan, collected a
few samples, remarking about their weight. In an attempt
to crush the samples, he found that the rock tended to
flatten rather than pulverize. Puzzled, but with an idea of
what they might have found, the men took the samples
with them. In Florence, Sullivan showed the samples to a
friend, Charles Mason, and apparently left one chunk,
without revealing the location of the find. Sullivan went on
west, and Mason quickly had the sample assayed. It proved
to be nearly pure silver chloride. Mason prospected along
the soldiers' route but failed to locate the outcrop.

Three years later, Mason and four friends were packing
ore out of the Globe area when they were attacked by
Apaches. One of the party was killed and his body buried on
the pass above Stoneman's Grade. An old road-camp oven
was utilized as a grave. After descending the grade, the
mules were put to water. One of the animals strayed and
was finally located on a knoll that held dark, dense outcrops of ore identical to those Sullivan had showed Mason

Collapse of the machine shed at Silver King Mine is imminent.

years before. The four men filed equal claims, and Silver King was born.

Two miles north, the Fortuna Mine opened up. An old Mexican wood hauler found that outcrop just under Fortuna Peak, while cutting wood for the Silver King. He sold it for $100.00 — $50 in cash, $50 in liquor.

In 1881, after millions in silver had been extracted from the original discovery, a man named Sullivan appeared at the site. He had been west to earn a stake so he could come back to work his discovery. To his amazement, a mine and town were built atop his find. He was graciously offered a job in the mill.

Mason and his friends eventually sold their shares in the mine. The first share went for $80,000, the second and third for somewhat more. The fourth partner held out for $300,000.

Between 1875 and 1888 the Silver King Mine took out $17

Company headquarters and guest house of the Silver King Mining Company was one of the first residential buildings in Arizona to have electricity.

million worth of silver. Most of it was refined at Pinal City. The stage carrying the bars was held up several times, the robbers escaping over the hills with the bars loaded on mules. The company solved that problem by pouring the silver out in bars too heavy to be toted by man or mule.

Silver King at its peak boasted two hotels, a combination church-school-dancehall, several saloons, and residences for 200 families. Now one is hard pressed to find even the foundations of most of the buildings. The large two-story company headquarters still stands on a knoll overlooking the collapsed remains of the machine shop. Down the hill a bit are two single-story rock buildings with plastered inside walls and tongue-and-groove wooden ceilings. Near the rock buildings, on a low hill, stands a small group of frame buildings.

Grace Middleton lives in one of these sunbleached structures near the entrance to town, a location necessary for the protection of her property. I happened to stop in just after she had had a run-in with some hippies who had made off with several windows — frames and all — from one of the old residences on the grounds. Her tone was distinctly cool as she told me of the windows and the recent theft of her camera and battery radio. She had been quite abrupt in her treatment of the vandals. She stood in the shade of her doorway, surrounded by her numerous dogs of various breed, and told me of her troubles, slowly graduating to the history of the town and ending with an expression of her deep affection for the place. As I listened, I made friends with the dogs. An hour later I was proud to be considered a friend of Grace Middleton, Queen of the Silver King.

MAP NOTE: The Superior, Arizona, United States Geological Survey 15 minute topographic map shows the area as it was in 1948. The 7½ minute map of the same name shows the Silver King area as it appeared at a later date, and in somewhat greater detail.

*Rock-walled and rock-roofed, this tiny house
was once home to a hard-rock miner.*

SONORA, ARIZONA

The old 1910 "Ray and Vicinity" map shows a number of satellite towns surrounding the coppertown of Ray. This map, revised in 1917 to correct for changes in "culture," shows no highways, only graveled roads. The Ray and Gila Valley Railroad Line is shown most prominently. The rail line reached Ray via the Mineral Creek Valley and terminated in a tangle of switchyards and sidetracks.

The mining of copper in 1917 was predominantly underground. A small open pit is shown between the "M and H" and the Tribunal shafts on the southwest slope of Humbolt Hill. The Ray, Madeline, Pearl Handle, Hecla, Sun, Flux, and Calumet shafts were all within the vicinity of town. The Burbank, Reed, Mineral, and Amanda tunnels bored into the hills a mile to the south.

The settlement called Ray (headquarters of the Ray Mining Company) was established in 1881 and named after the Ray Mine, which had earlier been given that name in honor of its discoverer's sister, Ray. The town proper was built in 1909 by the Hercules Copper Company. By 1915 satellite residential towns had sprung up around Ray. To the northwest were Boyd Heights and Americatown. To the southwest, Sonora and Barcelona occupied the gentle slopes leading to Sonora Hill.

Sonora was the largest of the group of satellites and, according to the map, was composed of sixty-odd square blocks. The town was established in 1912 by the Mexican employees of the Ray Consolidated Copper Company and was named (as were a great many Mexican mining camps) after the Mexican state of Sonora, on the Arizona border. Buildings lined the perimeters of the blocks. Courtyards were left in the center, in typical Spanish style. In the center of town, a four-square-block area was reserved for the town hall.

Emperor Hill once separated Ray and Sonora, but things have changed radically. The hill is now a deep pit, with boundaries that encroach upon the sites of all four of the surrounding towns. Barcelona and Sonora have been leveled but are yet to be excavated. The foundations and street patterns are still readily visible. On Sonora Hill, Kennecott Copper, the present operator of the mine, has built an overlook permitting a general view of the area. One has to stand on or climb over the fence in order to view the remains of the old towns — a practice frowned on by

Kennecott. A short hike around the south side of Sonora Hill to the old water tank will provide an excellent view of both townsites.

Just when the town of Sonora was leveled, is indefinite — at least the Arizona State Archives could provide no record of the event. That it is leveled is certain, and it's only a matter of time before the huge maws of the land-strippers eat their way through the site, removing all evidence of Sonora's existence.

MAP NOTE: The Ray and Vicinity, Arizona, 1910 United States Geological Survey topographic (special area) map shows all the old towns mentioned. The 1964 Sonora and Teapot Mountain, Arizona, 7½ minute maps show the same area, drastically changed by open-pit mining.

The remains of Sonora in the foreground will soon become part of the expanding open pit of the Kenecott Mine.

ARIZONA AREA 2

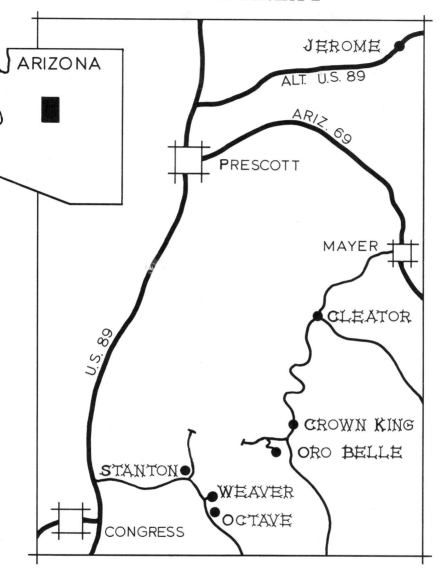

CLEATOR, ARIZONA

ON THE FLATS between Crazy Basin and Turkey Creek,
overlooked by Townsend Butte and Hercules Hill, are the
remnants of the once thriving town of Cleator.

Originally called Turkey, the town came into existence

The Turkey General Store (later to be named
Cleator) as it appeared in 1924.

in 1902 as a siding on the Prescott and Eastern Railroad.
The line was built southward from Mayer to the Crown
King Mine, first paralleling Cedar Canyon, then climbing
abruptly for twelve tortuous miles to the mines just under
7,100-foot Wasson Peak.

At the lower end of the grade, near the point where the
tracks crossed Turkey Creek, a siding was built to provide
service for the nearby Golden Turkey Mine. Later the siding also served the Golden Belt, St. John's, Gray Goose,
Silver Cord, and Golden Pheasant mines. In 1903 the siding
had accumulated a store, saloon, and a number of residences. That year the settlement was granted a post office
under the name of Turkey. L. P. Nellis ran the saloon and
store. He literally owned the town. He wasn't too happy
being a town-owner, often stating that he would rather
run cattle on his nearby spread than ride herd on his
saloon patrons.

*Updated photo shows the two main residential districts
of Cleator. Hospital is at upper left.*

James Patric Cleator, sailor turned prospector, stopped
by the saloon in 1905. Nellis and Cleator, over a drink or
two, developed a fast friendship. Within the day they had
formed a partnership which eventually found Cleator
running the store and Ellis the cattle.

The town grew as new mines opened. Within a dozen
years the population reached an estimated 1,500. An old
picture taken during this period shows more than sixty
substantial frame homes, with a second, uncountable
group of residences in a poorly focused background.

In 1925 the postal department, claiming confusion between Turkey and another similarly named post office,
requested a name change. James Patric Cleator (pronounced "Cleeter") was no doubt instrumental in choosing
the new name. Soon CLEATOR replaced TURKEY on the
saloon's false front.

During the late twenties and early thirties, the mines
closed down one after the other, stricken by the epidemic of
the depression. During the thirties a rock schoolhouse was
built with WPA labor, and the original school was converted to a residence.

When the railroad abandoned service in 1933, Cleator
suffered a second shrinkage. Most of the homes were
hauled away and the steel works of the mines scavenged
for scrap.

James Cleator became the sole owner of the remains of

Rock schoolhouse built with Works Progress Administration
(WPA) funds in the thirties.

One of the dozen or so residences that remain standing in Cleator.

the town, and in 1947 he decided to sell it — store, saloon, residences, and all. He promptly placed an ad in the *Arizona Republic*. The ad created a lot of interest and a sudden surge in business but failed to result in the sale of the town or any part of it. James Cleator died in 1959, and his son took over the town.

Today the store and a saloon remain with little change. The brands of gasoline and booze have changed. The town now has six or eight residents, according to a gentleman enjoying a cold drink at the store. He explained that the

The Cleator General Store as it appears today.

population estimate had to remain indefinite "'cause you don't know when someone goin' to the big city ain't coming back."

MAP NOTE: Cleator is shown on the Mayer, Arizona, 15 minute United States Geological Survey topographic map.

CROWN KING, ARIZONA

"Used to be more excitin' gettin' there than bein' there."
That's what the old-timer from near Mayer claimed. His
description of the road to Crown King, along the old railroad grade, included wild tales of driving the route in his
Model A Ford.

"Used to hang on the uphill side and keep nudgin' the
tires on the rails so's outside wheels wouldn't drop off the
ties." His descriptions were liberally seasoned with strings
of cusswords. Some combinations were as inventive as
they were unprintable.

"When they took the rails up — that's when it got a damn
site more hellish," he stated, then proceeded to explain
about the switchbacks.

"Those old switchbacks — they was the *original*
switchbacks." He zigzagged his hands. "They went like
that — no turns. Just drove into it, stopped, threw the
switch, then backed up to the next one, stopped, threw that
switch, then pulled ahead to the next."

He saw me taking notes. "You gonna print this?" I answered that I intended to. "Well, in that case, I'd rather
stay unanimous." I told him I'd vote for that. His eyes took
on a suspicious slant. He paused, shifted his teeth, and
then worked his way into another bunch of stories.

Mostly the old-timer talked about his prospecting days

*Triangular shape of Crown King was dictated by the railroad's turnaround
facility. Saloon is at center, general store is to the left.*

Jet streams overhead contrast with one of the oldest buildings in town.

down in Nevada, around Gold Point. In the process of getting some information about Crown King, I ended up with so many stories about Gold Point that I determined to enter that town on my "must visit" list.

I asked about the present condition of the road up to Crown King. "Tame — tame — wide as hell. Why they hauled a whole damn mill up there once, back when the road weren't so good."

The road was a delight. The magnificent view never failed to calm the mild case of nerves generally encountered on precarious paths. Of particular note were the narrow one-way rock cuts, unchanged from railroading days.

At first sight Crown King did not appear to fit the de-

The 1900 style of architecture common to mining towns is apparent even in this doghouse in Crown King.

scription of a ghost town. Too many people wandered about, and too many cars passed by. It's only after a complete tour that one can appreciate the number of old buildings remaining and subtract the effect of the remodeling and reuse of others.

The general store is still in business, little changed for nearly 100 years. Most of its trade is seasonal, and most of the traffic consists of vacationers attempting to elude the Arizona heat by escaping to the 7,000-foot altitude of the Bradshaw Mountains.

The old saloon looks exactly as an old saloon should. This venerable structure has had a number of names over the door, the most recent being "Andersons's and Van Tilborg's." Enough business remains in town to support a part-time barman, otherwise employed as a welder. It seems strange that a welder could make a living at his trade in this remote location, but dozens of small-time mining operations are still perking in the area. Jury-rigged equipment, assembled from secondhand parts, makes for frequent breakdowns and good business for the bartender-welder.

Gold was found in the Bradshaws in the early 1870s. The rush that followed, termed the "Bradshaw Excitement," resulted in the location of a number of paying mines. The Crown King was thought to be the finest but remained primarily a promoter's dream, due to the refractory nature (refusal to break down with heat) of the ore.

The miserable nature of the ore was noted early, and only the best was sorted out and sent to Prescott by mule train. Later the quality of the ore improved, giving cause for a railroad to be built. As was usually the case, the

General store in Crown King has been in business for almost 100 years.

Saloon, moved in from a neighboring town, once offered food, drink, and entertainment to the miners of Crown King. Outside stairway gave access to eight "going" rooms on second floor.

railroad brought prosperity to Crown King, and the population zoomed. There was no room for a roundhouse or circular turnaround. A triangular "back around" was built, utilizing the narrow creek beds that join at the townsite. The business part of town grew along one side of the triangle, and residences were built along the remaining legs.

The Crown King Mine closed in 1900, due to litigation. Continuing operations at the surrounding mines kept the town and railroad going. About 1910 the town of Crown King added two "used" saloons. Oro Belle, a few miles to the south, had lately become deserted. Its two saloons were dismantled and hauled by muleback over the steep, narrow trail connecting the two towns. Reassembled, the access to hard liquor improved, and the strict town rule against week-day drinking became an unenforceable blue law.

In the thirties, dumps at the Crown King Mine were

reworked. Assay reports showed that $2.5 million in gold could be reclaimed. Forgotten was the fact that this ore had been rejected as refractory. Half a million was invested in a new mill. Fifty men were hired, and the fading town of Crown King took on new life. Soon it was determined that the ore was resistant to the mill's best efforts. Managers were fired and new ones hired, yet the gap between assayed expectations and mill returns remained narrow — too narrow to allow profit. The mill closed. Some years later the post office was discontinued.

Perhaps Crown King's most interesting era was shortly after its regular train service was curtailed. During this period it is reported that autos, horses, foot traffic, and even occasional trains were using the same route. Automobiles frequently bounced down the ties, and passengers held their collective breath on the trestles.

The old duffer from Mayer had told me, "You could look down through those ties 200 feet — scare hell out of you. and after they took up the rails — the view got a damn site better!" He gave me a cornering look, and I figured he was about to give my leg a calculated tug. "You know, we used to go up to the dance there every Saturday night. The guy drivin' was supposed to stay sober, but we got to celebratin' and didn't keep count on him. We come down those tracks about dawn — 'course I wasn't seein' too good, but I'd swear we passed that train on the third switchback!"

MAP NOTE: Crown King and surrounding sites are shown on the Crown King, Arizona, 15 minute United States Geological Survey topographic map. Of interest are Lukes Hoist, Oro Belle, Fort Misery, and the Horse Thief Basin Recreation Area.

Old mill ruins and boardinghouses reflect the light of a full moon.

ORO BELLE, ARIZONA

From Crown King an excellent gravel road heads south. In a half mile a branch heads west, and in another mile a jeep road angles toward the south. A sign indicates that Oro Belle is three miles away in that direction — but also warns that passenger cars should not attempt it. Actually it is a fairly good jeep road but somewhat narrow for a full-sized pickup. I swallowed hard and often for two of those three miles.

Oro Belle once occupied both legs of a switchback. Now only a few shacks and tanks can be found on the uphill stretch. Across the gully and down the other side of the switchback are a number of old buildings, all of the ghostly quality that totally befits a completely deserted town. The most outstanding is a large rock structure — probably the mine office and company store. It has fancy, embossed metal trim in both scroll and brick design. One wall leans out over the road, making it nearly impassable. Behind this building, and implying that more substantial build-

Remains of Oro Belle are almost hidden by the lush growth.
Mine above town is the Rapid Transit.

Fancy structure was probably company office and bank combination. Tilting wall at right allows little room to pass.

ings once existed, is a rock wall more than 150 feet long. Built into this wall is a vault, its door missing, reportedly stolen in the past few years. Apparently a bank or more company buildings once fronted the wall. To the south are several old frame buildings. The cupola above one of them would indicate it had a need to expel unwanted heat, which would make it an assay office or possibly a cook shack.

Somewhere along the lower main street were located two saloons, a few stores, a deputy sheriff's office, and a justice of the peace court. For all this law enforcement, it would be reasonable to assume that a sporting house or two also flourished here, although available history concerning the town makes no mention of such establishments.

In the late 1890s George P. Harrington obtained title to some claims in the area. He shortly organized the Oro Belle Mining and Milling Company and proceeded to sell stock. By 1900 the mines had proved their worth, and a mill was built to process ore from the Oro Belle and the Gray

Stick by stick, the two saloons of Oro Belle were
hauled up the mountain to Crown King.

Eagle. The population of the town reached 200, with 100 of them miners. Forty men worked the day shift on the Oro Belle.

Nearby, the Rapid Transit and Savoy mines were operating, although in less spectacular fashion. A post office was granted the town, and the temporary name of Harrington was changed to Oro Belle. George Harrington proved to be too nice a fellow, according to the company stockholders. They objected to his using company funds to grubstake prospectors. He was fired, and a new boss of the penny-pinching variety was hired. Shortly a revolt was mounted, and the new boss was given an ultimatum — better food and better pay or no work. Elsewhere such miners' revolts had resulted in the burning of mills and occasionally the suspension of the boss — by the neck!

The demands were granted, but, within weeks, miners' wages were cut back and the quality of the meals sank to a new low.

The second revolt was more serious. A few ropes were visible. The demands were restated. The badly shaken

Vacant interior of this structure makes speculation concerning its function rather difficult, but cupola implies use as cook shack, assay office, or smithy.

manager conceded. He set off immediately to purchase fresh meat and produce. He never returned.

Mines in the area reached the extent of their lodes in 1910. The good ore was gone, and the low-grade that was left wouldn't pay wages, let alone milling fees.

Soon both of Oro Belle's saloons were dismantled and hauled muleback to Crown King. In 1918 the post office closed. The only signs of life now are a few rattlers and a number of lizards — the latter frequently raising the pulse of visitors momentarily convinced they are confronted by the former.

MAP NOTE: The Crown King, Arizona, 15 minute United States Geological Survey topographic map shows Oro Belle and a great number of old mines in the surrounding mountains.

JEROME, ARIZONA

Compared to deserted Oro Belle, Jerome is like Sunday on the freeway. However, the degree of desertion in the two towns is similar. Oro Belle is 100 per cent deserted and Jerome 98 per cent, having shrunk from its 1929 peak of 15,000 to its present two or three hundred stubborn souls. Clinging to the thirty-degree slope of Cleopatra Hill, with its upper end 1,500 feet higher than its lower, the town compactly occupies both sides of a number of switchbacks. The back side of a building may face one leg of the main highway, and the front will face another.

Since 1925, when a 250-pound charge of dynamite was touched off underground, many of the buildings have been sliding slowly down the hill — some buildings at a rate of three-eighths of an inch per month! The jail has slid a number of feet (some claim 300 feet) and across a highway. Three hundred feet is unbelievable, but so is the way people trust their houses to stay put and not slip down the hill in the middle of the night. Residents are seeeminly uncon-

Jerome clings tenaciously to the eastern slope of Cleopatra Hill.

Built by the pastor and parishioners, this church was constructed largely of old powder boxes, then covered with stucco.

cerned with their near-perpendicular life and continue to drive their automobiles into rooftop garages and climb down to their living rooms.

More than a thousand years ago the Tuzigoot Indians dug into the side of the hill to glean the brightly hued green and blue oxides of copper. The pigment was highly valued as body ornamentation and pottery coloring. The metallic content was not noted or valued. Even the Spaniards who visited the sites in the sixteenth century failed to become interested in the copper, for their interest was gold.

Several prospectors filed claims here in 1876. M. A. Ruffner and Angus (or August) McKinnon proved up on their claims then sold out to Territorial Governor Tritle for $2,000. The governor sought financial help and found it in Eugene Jerome, a cousin of Winston Churchill. Mr. Jerome set down the stipulation that the town must bear his name. Previous to that time, the settlement had been called Eureka or Wade Hampton, for two of the earliest claims. The former was the Greek word for "I found it," and the latter the name of the governor of South Carolina.

First attempts to produce pure copper from the ore proved disappointing, and the mines were sold to William A. Clark, a Montana millionaire. Under his direction the United Verde grew to a profitable and complex operation. William Clark became one of the richest men in America and a United States Senator — and he did it, please note, in that order.

Wide wheels of heavy-duty wagon frame the powderhouse church of Jerome. Large buildings above are the abandoned grade school and hospital.

*Little Daisy Hotel as seen from the Daisy Mine. Hotel
was home to single miners in the area.*

At one time the town boasted four grocery stores, eight
houses of joy, seventeen saloons, and two churches. The
miners maintained their usual priorities.

The population of Jerome began to decline during the
depression, but in 1935 the Phelps Dodge Corporation
bought the operation for $20 million. Many thought the
purchase ill-advised, but by 1940, when the deposits
thinned, the company had netted a profit of $40 million.
The figure seems substantial, but it represents only a

small fraction of the $1 billion worth of copper, gold, silver, and zinc taken out of Cleopatra Hill.

MAP NOTE: Details of the town and its environs can be pinpointed, and an all-inclusive tour laid out, with the aid of the Clarkdale and Mingus Mountain, Arizona, 15 minute topographic maps. It seems only fitting that a town that sits on the steep slope that joins mountain to plain is also found split in half — part on one map, the remainder on another.

Intent of sign on old home is not clear. Either humans should beware of vermin, or vermin should beware of the danger of a sudden slip downhill.

STANTON, ARIZONA

Pauline Weaver, in the year 1962, undertook to guide a group of prospectors into the hills of central Arizona. He was a half-breed army scout temporarily off the payroll. His ability to negotiate and communicate with the Apaches made up for the fact that he had never been in the area before.

One evening an antelope was shot and butchered and camp set up beside a nearby creek. This rather mundane series of events had happened before, but this time one little item would be added that would cause the stream to be named Antelope Creek and another stream Weaver Creek. The hill above camp would become famous as Rich

Large stage station, store, and residence are the only remains of Stanton, site of frequent foul play.

Hill. Two thousand miners would flood the vicinity, and four towns would spring into being. The event? Their stock strayed, and some of the party went in search. As in many cases, the mules made the discovery. When the men found the stock they also found several thousand dollars' worth of gold nuggets.

The camp became permanent and was given the name of Antelope, later to be called Antelope Station when the stage line passed through. Somewhat later that name would change to Stanton by means of a series of crimes, including at least four murders.

In the meantime a town a few miles east, settled mostly by Mexicans, would be named in honor of Weaver. The town was to degenerate quickly into an outlaw hideout. Octave, beyond Weaver, would grow to a more substantial town, with the steadying influence of a deep shaft bearing gold in quartz. Congress Junction, to the west, would grow up as a supply station for the Rich Hill Mining District.

Charles P. Stanton arrived in Antelope Station, having recently been thrown out of a monastery on a morals charge. He obtained a decent job in spite of his record but soon became disenchaned with his status as deputy county recorder and began to plot his way to success.

He envied two successful storekeepers in the community, and by the diligent planting of rumors and counterrumors, he got Partridge and Wilson angry with each other. Things boiled over when a hog got into Patridge's cabin. Wilson was on his way to the cabin to apologize on behalf of his partner, the hog's owner. Stanton saw his opportunity and quickly had a Mexican cohort run to tell Partridge that Wilson was gunning for him. As a result, Partridge shot Wilson dead on sight. He was tried and found guilty, partly on the basis of his confession, which Stanton helpfully wrote out for him.

Wilson's partner, Timmerman, took over the store. Soon Timmerman's body was found along the road. Stanton promptly moved the stage route so that it passed his own store and erected a large sign which, in essence, renamed the town Stanton.

Charles Stanton was still not content. He now envied Barney Martin, for Barney was still the stage agent. Barney was told by some members of the Valenzuel gang from Weavertown that he had better move out or he and his family would die. Barney sold out, packed up, and headed for Phoenix, leaving word with a good friend at Cold Water

Powder house just east of Stanton once had stout metal door. Short wooden door poses a mystery.

Station that he would stop by on the way. When Barney failed to arrive, his friend, Captain Calderwood, went in search. He found the charred remains of the wagon and family. The Valenzuel gang was suspected, and Stanton was thought to be their leader. Stanton was tried for murder but found innocent. It is appropriate that when Stanton finally died it was by the hand of another outlaw and for "moral" reasons. He had made advances toward Froilana, a young Mexican girl and close relative of Lucero, leader of a second gang in Weaver.

Tom Pierson, on the way down from Crown King, re-

*Adjacent to powder house, giant saguaro cactus
overlooks an area noted for rattlers.*

ported that he met the fleeing Lucero. "I've killed Stanton
and I'm headed for the border," stated Lucero as he rode
past.

"Stick around," hollered Pierson. "We'll get you a re-
ward."

The ghost town of Stanton is about a mile and a half
north and six miles east of Congress Junction. No topographic maps are available for any of the towns in the
vicinity. Three rather large buildings mark the site of the
old town, but they have to be viewed from a distance. The
area is surrounded with "No" signs: No Trespassing, No
Prospecting, No Filing of Claims and, at an occupied residence a few hundred yards to the north, a sign crowded in
among more "No" signs proclaims, "Beware of the dog." I
would have given ten bucks for a sign reading "Welcome to
Stanton," and another five for the privilege of planting it
at the outskirts of town.

MAP NOTE: No United States Geological Survey topographic maps are
available for the area.

WEAVER, ARIZONA

Established in 1862 and all washed up by 1900, the little town of Weaver led a short but varied life. It was named in honor of the scout who led the discovery party, Pauline Weaver. Weaver was the half-breed son of a white father and an Indian mother, the daughter of a tribal chief. Weaver was a highly respected army scout who had aided General Kearny in several Western campaigns. He died, reportedly from the shifting of a long-buried arrowhead, while asleep in an Indian camp on the outskirts of Camp Lincoln in 1867.

Weaver was the biggest placer find in Arizona's history. More than a million dollars' worth of coarse gold was separated from the gravel of Weaver Creek, and untold smaller fortunes were literally picked off the ground on the upper slopes of Rich Hill. In 1888 the camp had reached its mining

Two buildings of mixed construction probably housed gold-washing equipment.

peak. An old photograph shows twenty substantial wooden buildings, a few rock and adobe structures, three large gravel-washers, and thirty tents. By the 1890s the gold-washing business was fading, and hell-raising was taking over. Before long the town had the reputation of being an outlaw haven. In fact, it is claimed that no lawman dared set foot in Weaver, lest he disappear without a trace. Several gangs of outlaws operated out of the town in open fashion, frequently hired by outsiders like Stanton, to do some choice dirty work. Murders were common in town and seldom recorded. The cemetery had a number of unmarked mounds. William Segna, in 1898, had the honor of being the last murder victim in Weaver. He was a well-to-do saloon and mercantile operator — too well-to-do.

Respectability returned temporarily in 1899 when the town was granted a post office. However, due to a sudden loss in population (everyone moved two miles away to Octave), the post office was closed down in less than a year.

Weaver's tiny post office, built in 1899, shows wide variation in the size of rocks used in its construction.

*Burned-out residence at east edge of Weaver overlooks slopes of
Rich Hill, known for its numerous gold nuggets.*

The remains of Weaver can be found by traveling two miles east of Stanton, then taking a road north for a mile. The branch road to the north leaves the main road just short of the town of Octave.

The old Weaver post office is still standing and in pretty good shape. The building had two rooms — one for customers, one for the postmaster. The rock walls are twenty-four inches thick, considerably reducing the available room inside but insuring a cool environ. The rock walls appear to have been laid up by two different workmen — one stout and one of lesser strength. The rocks on the south side are huge, and those on north are small. The doorway forms the demarkation.

Several other rock buildings, an adobe structure with tin roof, two old frame mine shacks, and a concrete vault complete the standing remains. The vault is at the north end of town and seems to have been poured over a form shaped like a narrow-gage railroad car, then the form removed from the inside. The form wood was narrow, fluted wainscoating, as evidenced by the fancy imprint left in the concrete.

At the south end of town, on a hill to the east, stands the burned hulk of a small farmhouse. Alongside the remains is the charred trunk of a tree that once offered the home a moment of noonday shade.

MAP NOTE: No topographic maps are available for the area.

OCTAVE, ARIZONA

C. O. Carlson is presently the sole resident of Octave. You might call him a new-fangled type of old-timer. He used to prospect extensively. Now he has formed a company that plans to extract gold from the reject ore that makes up the waste dumps of the fabulous old Octave Mine. C. O. figures a million in gold sits on the dump awaiting an efficient extraction system. And he figures he's got just the gadget to do the job. In fact, he has applied for a patent on his new-style ball mill. It's the drive mechanism that makes it unique. The rear end and transmission of a twenty-ton truck — wheels, tires and all — is rammed up against the large armor-plate drum. The air in the tires can be adjusted to achieve proper contact. C. O. enjoys turning the driveshaft with one hand, pointing out the easy rotation the drum makes as a result. "This mill will run 200 tons

Mill ruins mark the site of the old Octave Mine, the only mine in the area to successfully tap an underground gold vein.

easy," he claimed. I didn't ask if that was per hour, day, or week, but I sure had to agree it was a beautiful piece of eyeball engineering.

"Of course," I pointed out, "that drum is going to be somewhat tougher to turn when you get a few tons of ore in it."

Carlson figured, perhaps a bit optimistically, that he could drive the loaded mill with as little as twenty horsepower. There is no such thing as a pessimistic inventor.

Ore from the dump is to be treated first in a jaw crusher, then put through the ball mill with fifty gallons of water a minute added. The fine gold mixed powdered rock will run out the end onto a couple of fanners (shaker tables). Finally, part of the gold will be gravity-separated and the remainder extracted by chemical means.

C. O. is well-acquainted with the history of the place and the exact condition of the old Octave Mine. Where he got his information is a mystery to me, and it differs from the

C. O. Carlson checks drive mechanism on
ball mill of his own unique design.

Diamond-shaped water reservoir, built of rock in 1897 and still intact, is one of Octave's more durable remnants.

published material one can dig out of the Arizona State Library. In several cases I have found C. O. to be right and the published record in error. For example, one writer claims the town had a population of 3,000. Since others state that the entire district had only 2,000 maximum, I'm inclined to put stock in Carlson's claim that the town had about 500 residents, mostly Scandinavians.

The diamond-shaped water reservoir in the center of town was built of rock in 1879. The buildings nearby were built about 1900. Now, just the rock foundations remain. The business district held a post office, mine headquarters, saloon, mercantile, and grocery. There was also a school and a building that served as bank and stage station. C. O. claims there were 150 men on the digging crew in the Octave Mine and that the mine was 2,400 feet deep. Pumps ran continually to keep the lower 2,000 feet dewatered!

"Of course the mine is flooded now — there's 20 miles of tunnels under that water, and I don't guess it will ever be pumped," said Carlson. "See that hill over there? That's Rich Hill — richest hill in the world. Why, after a rain you can walk up there and find nuggets. People still search around that hill — find stuff too, especially just over the crest." Carlson was warming up to the subject now. "The geologists never did figure out how all those nuggets got to be found on top of the hill — supposed to find 'em in the streams below."

C. O. pointed to the south. "See that peak? That's Vulture Peak. Had a good ore body down there. We're on a line between that mine and Rich Hill. That's why they found so much gold here."

I asked how the snakes were. Carlson answered to the effect that they were real healthy. "In fact, the damn things are so fat they're pink! They must be the most beautiful rattlers in the world. And they don't buzz — must have killed off all the buzzing kind and grew a crop that don't buzz!"

C. O. is inclined to be outspoken on matters political. "It's that L-208 — you know, Law No. 208 that Roosevelt put through — that's what killed this mine — and those old

Some of Octave's rock foundation, still solidly in place, was laid up without mortar.

tinheads in Congress soaked it all in. Never should have stopped everybody from minin' gold — just 'cause they claimed it wasn't strategic."

C. O. doesn't hold with core drilling either — "Why you can drill those little bitty holes all month and still miss the vein. It's crazy! May as well take your money to Vegas."

There are some facts concerning the town that C. O. overlooked. He probably knows them but just had more important things to say.

Claimed as a placer in 1864, nothing much happened until the 1890s when someone saw the deep-mine potential. Eight men got together, bought the claim, and named the place Octave, appropriate to the eight-way split. No information is available as to how long the original eight held on to the claim. It would have meant a fortune for

Gold was melted and poured into ingots at the bullion house across the road from the Octave Mine and Mill.

each, since somewhere between $8 and $15 million in gold was eventually extracted from the Octave.

The town proper was built between 1896 and 1901. The post office moved in from Weaver in 1900. The mines were shut down in 1942, due to L-208, and in 1944 all the buildings were razed to save on taxes. Visible today are the huge yellow tailings of the mill, some foundations, some walls of the bullion room, the reservoir, and extensive multileveled rock foundations. Across the knoll, under a modern power line, is a totally forgotten cemetery.

I had just visited the cemetery and was swinging back through the site of Octave to say goodbye to C. O. when I was hailed down by a nondescript old character in a battered pickup. "Where's Rich Hill?" he asked. "It's got to be around here somewhere."

Like an old hand and long-time resident I waved toward the hill and hollered, "Your best bet for nuggets is just over the crest — too bad it ain't rained lately."

MAP NOTE: No topographic maps are presently available for the area.

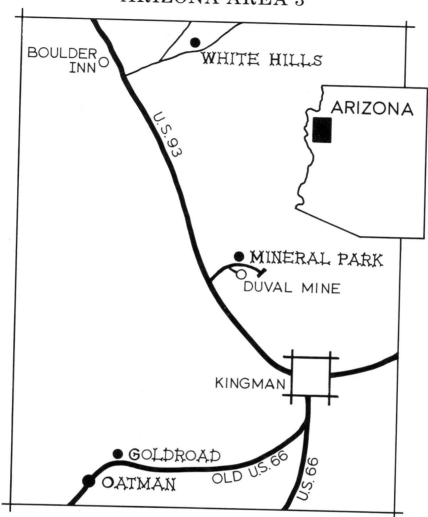

GOLDROAD, ARIZONA

THE ROAD FROM KINGMAN slants southwest with little
change in direction or elevation. Occasionally it dips to
accommodate a dry wash. The native knows enough to
slow down and check the wash for water. The tourist might
plow into two feet of water at fifty miles per hour, but he'll
only do it once. The resulting baptism quickly makes one a
native.

*Lower Goldroad is covered with roofless remains
of rock walls, stores, and residences.*

After fifteen miles the road angles west and proceeds to
meander another ten miles up the slope to Sitgreaves Pass,
3,750 feet above sea level. Its famed "100-mile view" is now
marred at mid-distance by the smoke of a huge electrical
generating plant located on the Colorado River.

As the road writhes its way down the west slope, signs of
the abandoned town of Goldroad appear. Here a tunnel,
there an old rock foundation. Beyond these, a shaft and
gallows frame. The switchbacks become more frequent,

*Two-story adobe hotel, now in shambles, once stood
proudly at the center of Goldroad.*

and at one point, where the grade is particularly steep,
most of deserted Goldroad is visible straight ahead and
sharply below.

Most of the remains are rock or adobe walls. Assured
that the town would never come to life again, the owners
decided in 1949 to save the tax on surface improvements
and intentionally burned the town to the ground. The Mexican part of town, on the treeless flat to the west, survived
in part, due to its adobe construction.

Traces of gold were found here in 1863. The outcrops
were low grade, and the prospectors moved on. The gold

Goldroad was burned down to save taxes. Wooden roofs burned, but door and window casements somehow survived.

was there but remained hidden for another fifty-three years.

Jose Jeres (Jenerez, according to the February 1916 *Los Angeles Financial News*) was grubstaked by Henry Lovin of Kingman to the extent of $1,300. Jerez, or Jenerez, headed into the thoroughly worked-over region near Sitgreaves Pass, by the Old Fort Mohave Military Road. The stories vary — but Jose was either tracking a lost burro or tying one up when he stumbled across a knobby outcrop. He chipped some samples, then quickly laid out his claim, and headed for Kingman.

Lovin wouldn't believe Jerez when he learned the "strike" was in an area already tramped over by a

Grout-and-rock staircase leads nowhere.

thousand prospectors, and it wasn't until Jerez started asking for another stake that Lovin decided to go look. Jerez was right, and excitedly the two of them proceeded to dig the required hole to prove up the claim. The vein held steady and strong. The ore assayed at $1,200 per ton.

Word got out, and the rush was on. The ground was gone over thoroughly a second time. Two other paying shafts were developed. Meanwhile, Lovin and Jerez sold out for $25,000 each. Lovin also got the freighting and mercantile concessions, which paid handsomely. Jerez drank his

Desert flora has its own distinctive beauty.

share and within a few years departed this world by swallowing rat poison.

In 1901 there were 400 people in town. In 1902 the boom was well under way, and a post office was opened under the name of Acme. In 1906 the town reached its peak. That year the post office was redesignated as Goldroad. It remained so until 1941, when Law 208 closed down the mine, the town, and the post office. Around the bend, and two miles on down the highway, is the delightful old town of Oatman. Although not as dead as some ghost town buffs desire, one can couple it with the more-than-dead remnant of Goldroad and come up with an enjoyable tour.

MAP NOTE: The town, important mines, and cemetery are shown on the Oatman and Mt. Nutt 7½ minute United States Geological Survey topographic maps.

OATMAN, ARIZONA

The geology of the area would excite even the most dejected prospector. Igneous intrusions stand boldly above the surface. Quartz outcrops abound — and where there is quartz, there is the likelihood of valuable mineralization. Quartz, one of the last minerals to solidify upon cooling, often carries rare metals in its cracks and fissures. To the east of Oatman, the nearly white Elephant's Tooth and black Boundary Cone thrust their way above the horizon, sure signs of mineral separation and reliable indicators of valuable deposits nearby.

The Vivian Mine was located in 1902 by Ben Paddock. A mine camp grew up around it, and in 1904 the post office of Vivian was established. The population reached 150, and the town boasted two banks, two stores, and a chamber of commerce.

Discovery of rich gold ore in the Tom Reed Mine in 1908 brought the first boom. The town grew and became so respectable that a move was made to select a new name. They decided on Oatman, in honor of a family of pioneers who had been attacked by Indians in 1851. The entire family was killed, except for two girls and a boy. The girls were taken captive and the boy left for dead at the site of

Empty remains of the Lee Lumber Company and the Oatman Picture Show bracket the north entrance to Oatman, Arizona. Large quartz outcrop thrusting above horizon is named the Elephant's Tooth.

Front of Oatman's Lee Lumber Company viewed from covered walk of deserted picture show building.

the massacre. A rescue party found the boy and, after years of effort, managed to free one of the girls. The other sister died in captivity.

George W. Long had a theory about the veins around

South end of Oatman's nearly deserted Main Street. Building at right was originally a drugstore and soda shop. Memorial in the center of intersection is to Anna Eder, beloved citizen known for grubstaking most of the prospectors in the area. Although she died penniless, she once had sizable income from town property which included most of the Oatman's red-light district.

Lower terminal of aerial tramway ends at the headquarters of the Tom Reed Mine at east edge of Oatman.

Oil barrel rode the tramway continuously. Small cogwheel below right wheel drove pump that lifted oil from the drum to the cable.

Oatman. He studied the shafts and tunnels in existence and determined that a healthy vein of gold ran north and south about 380 feet below ground. He formed the United Eastern Mining Company, which in 1913 bought up a number of claims that included the theoretical streak of gold. He was right. The vein was there — and at the depth predicted. With the Eastern and the Tom Reed both producing well (the Tom Reed averaged $70,000 in gold per month) the town boomed, and the area's population neared the 10,000 mark. Later a figure of 15,000 was claimed, but this was probably an exaggeration.

With the best ore removed, the mines went into slow decline during the thirties. The town began to shrink. Its life was sustained by its location on Route 66. Even the Oakies passing through to California did their share to contribute to the survival of Oatman.

But Law 208, passed by "those tin heads in Congress" (to quote C. O. Carlson of Octave, Arizona), brought the remaining gold mining to a halt. The number of residents

Now the Glory Hole, Oatman's old drugstore was recently "gussied up" for a role in the movie "How the West Was Won."

dropped to one hundred or so and in 1968 fell to half that, or less than one percent of its "honest" peak population.

There are a few more folk living in Oatman now. In fact it may be on the comeback as a winter residence for retired trailerites, following the sun south for the winter but fleeing the Arizona heat each summer.

The old Tom Reed Mine and Mill, long idle, has enough property remaining to warrant a caretaker. A few mines in the area are still operating, either on a one-man basis or under strict secrecy. In one case the secrecy is maintained by a rifle-carrying guard.

Wild burros make it a habit to visit town each day. Somewhere between six and twenty of them wander in for a tour of the stores, poking their heads into doors and walking in if not met at the threshold. They like popcorn and dog food, and the tourists love to provide it, even at the risk of nipped fingers. The burros are descendants of the pack animals turned loose by retired prospectors. They are

Wild burros make daily forays along Oatman's Main Street. Favorite snacks include popcorn and dog food.

If snacks are not offered on the street, burros will walk into stores to beg at the counter. Grace Kloehn, proprietor of a glass shop, heads Blackjack off at the door.

not completely tame. Fights for herd supremacy some-times occur on the main street. Storekeepers close their doors, while visitors take cover and grab for their In-stamatics.

Occasionally samples of high-grade ore appear in the glass showcases of the grocery store. I was offered a chunk about the size of a marshmallow. It was perhaps five to ten percent gold. You could easily scratch the yellow portion with a knife blade to check that it was not pyrite. The sample probably had an eighth of an ounce of gold in it. The price was $10. Too high, I figured, and passed it up. Later, halfway to Kingman, it dawned on me that, at the present $180 an ounce, that sample was probably worth twice the asking price.

MAP NOTE: The Oatman, Arizona, 7½ minute United States Geological Survey topographic map shows Oatman and part of Goldroad.

MINERAL PARK, ARIZONA

You can see the plume of dust from ten miles away. The closer you approach, the more it seems to rise from the exact site of the ghost town of Mineral Park. A mile away you can hear the hum and clatter of heavy machinery. On a rise to the south of the suspiciously smooth, broad, gravel road is an old roofless adobe building, doubtless a remnant of Mineral Park.

Just around the bend the noise becomes suddenly louder, and the field of view is filled with signs of "progress." The Duval Mine and Mill is operating at a level that would have been beyond the imagination of residents of Mineral Park ninety years ago.

The site is a study in contrasts. On the left side of the road are the pitiful wrecks of three or four buildings, some mill foundations, one head frame about to collapse, and an old wooden separation tank. From these relics you can look across to the monstrous mine dump of the Duval, matched

Keystone Mine stands over the remains of one of the mills at Mineral Park. Cerbat Mountains form the backdrop.

*Head frame of the Keystone Mine is about to collapse of its own weight.
Massive tailings behind are from the still-active Duval Mine.*

only in size by the massive mill below. Periodically the ugly sound of rocks falling causes one to look quickly about. The trucks are dumping rock over the dump a mile away, and boulders the size of barrels roll hundreds of feet down the man-made talus slope.

A brief history, to match the meager extent of the remains, starts with the town being laid out in 1870 near a five-stamp mill. There were seven saloons in operation within six months. The big boom of the 1880s found many adobe and frame buildings built on both sides of a wide main street. A flagpole stood at the uphill end. An old picture shows wagon ruts forming a series of figure eights as people drove to the front of each store, then cut across to one on the other side of the street.

In 1884 the population was 700 and increasing. There were two newspapers and a Chinatown. Strangely, there were no banks and no churches. Perhaps a basic truth was evident. Without one, perhaps you have a lesser need of the other.

When the Atlantic and Pacific tracks were laid along a route just fourteen miles away, it was found that ore of lesser quality could be mined. The town took on new life — temporarily. Soon a junction town popped into existence at the loading site. Within three years that town exceeded Mineral Park in size. An election showed that the majority approved of the new town as the county seat. Mineral Park refused to give up the records. A midnight raid solved the problem. The new town went on to become a success — they named it Kingman.

MAP NOTE: The 1939, 15 minute Chloride, Arizona, United States Geological Survey topographic map shows the site of Mineral Park, but gives no indication of the present mining complex.

Remains of Mineral Park's second mill, built about 1874, appear insignificant when viewed against the gigantic Duval Mill.

*The last structure in White Hills slowly eases
its way toward the horizontal.*

WHITE HILLS, ARIZONA

Silver was found here in 1892, and by 1894 the White
Hills Mining Company had built a town and a mill and had
dug twenty-seven miles of tunnels. The mines were paying
handsomely, and the fifteen hundred residents in the area
didn't mind the occasional gully washer that rushed down
the White Hills and floated away an outhouse or two. What
they did mind was the shortage of drinking water and its
"hauled-in" price!

The White Hills Mining Company fell into financial difficulty, and an English outfit took over in 1895. A seven-mile
pipe brought springwater to town and supplied the needs
of a new forty-stamp mill. Most of the water went to the
mill, and the town folk still felt the shortage.

In two years the original owners regained the property,
due to the English outfit's inability to make the payments.

Barrel cactus volunteers as headboard in the old cemetery of White Hills.

A big promotional effort was started, and the town experienced its best year. Then, with thinning veins and with promotional claims unfulfilled, the mines and White Hills began to fade.

A bad flood wiped out much of the town. Men caught 200 feet underground could not climb out against the water and debris pouring in. Luckily, the shaft went deeper and acted as a reservoir, or the men would have been trapped and drowned.

The post office closed in 1914, but by then most of the town had been moved away or had collapsed from flood-damaged foundations.

Until recently, several old shacks still remained, stubbornly fighting the pull of gravity. A new retirement village, built a few miles beyond the site, did little to protect the meager remains. In 1974 the last shack collapsed to a point where its eaves touched the ground.

The cemetery has a number of graves, each lined with rocks, a few replete with accidental barrel cactus headboards. The ultimate insult to a dead town is sickeningly evident there. Two graves have been dug up and robbed. One of them was that of a child.

MAP NOTE: The White Hills, Arizona, 15 minute United States Geological Survey topographic map shows the site.

PART III
NEVADA

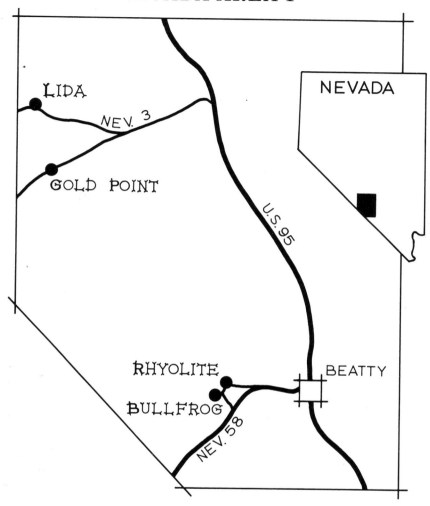

BULLFROG, NEVADA

SHORTY HARRIS had never made a big stake. He had made
a strike or two, but somehow it always seemed to slip
through his fingers. The finds that he kept always turned
out shallow, and the ones he sold made the buyer rich.
There was always the next one, and that one he would
handle right, for Shorty figured he had used up all the
wrong ways.

Late in the summer of 1904, Shorty Harris and his friend,

Ernest Cross, split off from a group of prospectors at Daylight Springs in southern Nevada and headed west to a spot Shorty had noted some years earlier. On August 4 the two prospectors found some greenish rock containing imbedded quartz, and in the quartz were granular chunks of gold. Smooth portions of the rock resembled the back of a bullfrog. They ground up some of the rock and panned out the gold. It was rich as any ore they had ever seen — and this time it wasn't someone else holding on to it. This could be the big one!

Harris and Cross checked the area closely and staked out the best deposits — then, with foresight, staked out a millsite and and water rights. They loaded up all the samples they could and headed for Goldfield. On the way they stopped at Beatty's Ranch, and word of the strike began to spread. It spread so fast that one newspaper reporter claimed the two men met prospectors coming at them from Goldfield when they were still ten miles out and that when the two discoverers reached Goldfield, all of Goldfield was staking claims near the Bullfrog. The story is only slightly

Adobe walls mark the site of Bullfrog's once-busy Main Street.

*Hot sun has curled the shingles on roof of shack
at the site of original Bullfrog claim.*

exaggerated, for 7,000 people were on the site within a few months.

Shorty's credit was good at every bar in Goldfield, and he exercised his prerogative in all of them. Later he claimed that six days of drinking too much "Oh-Be-Joyful" had addled his brain! He didn't remember signing the deed, but there it was — with seven witnesses. He had sold his half of The Bullfrog for $1,000! Another stake had slipped from his grasp.

Later Shorty claimed it was $25,000, probably in an attempt to sound as astute as his partner, Ernest Cross, who had held out for that figure. His partner claimed that Shorty had sold his interest for just $400; others claimed it was $500 and a mule. The latter version isn't likely, since Shorty hated mules, much preferring jackasses. In fact, his gravestone was later to be inscribed: "Here Lies Shorty Harris, A Single Blanket Jackass Prospector." Shorty became famous as the best and the poorest prospector in the southwest. Wherever he went, he left a trail of riches behind.

The Bullfrog strike was made in August, and by November nearly a dozen tent towns had sprung up, some near the original claim and others scattered about the flats near Ladd Mountain a few miles to the east.

Water had to be hauled in. Freighting costs made it nearly equal in price to unaged whiskey. That made hard

*Paint has protected portions of an otherwise sandblasted
headboard in Fullfrog's cemetery. Raised
letters read in part, "Anderson 1906."*

liquor a bargain by comparison. It was in such demand
that many of the shipments were intercepted enroute and
consumed on the spot. It was common practice to set up
shop at the point of interception. It was several months
before the open-air bars satisfied the demand and were
able to migrate to the mining camps.

Land promoters attempted to lure residents to "their"
towns in order to sell lots at a profit. To get things started
they all offered free lots, and some escalated the competition with the offer of free house-moving. The shifting of

Ornate headstone in Bullfrog's cemetery marks grave of Daniel G. Kennedy, born in Antigonish County, Nova Scotia. Kennedy and Bullfrog died the same year.

homes and relocation of business places finally slowed as two dominant towns emerged: Bullfrog, on the flat south of Sutherland Mountain, and Rhyolite, a mile to the north.

Promoters of both towns knew that only one could survive. The competition was heavy. Each town built to match the other — and by May 30, 1905, both had large hotels, water systems, newspapers, and post offices.

Within a year Rhyolite emerged as the winner. It was a more substantial town with a number of two-and three-story rock buildings under construction. Lots in Bullfrog dropped in value, and stores along its main street became vacant. When the last business place moved to Rhyolite, the *Rhyolite Herald* proclaimed: "Verily the Bullfrog Croaketh."

That was in May of 1906, and in June of the same year the big three-story hotel in Bullfrog burned to the ground. The town had boomed and collapsed in less than two years.

The map of the area indicates the ruins of two buildings and a cemetery at the site of Bullfrog. It is totally accurate. The road to the west, part of it atop the old railroad grade, leads to the collapsed structures of the original Bullfrog Mine. Of the mine shafts there, some are caved in, others are filled with the debris of fallen buildings.

MAP NOTE: The Bullfrog, Nevada, 15 minute topographic map of the United States Geological Survey shows Bullfrog, the Discovery Mine, and other settlements in the area.

RHYOLITE, NEVADA

When Bullfrog "croaked" in 1906, the population of Rhyolite increased by several hundred. The first of three railroads reached town the same year, and Rhyolite took a second giant step forward.

The town was exploding much faster than profits from the mines warranted. Mine stocks were high-priced and selling fast. People who had arrived too late for the Goldfield boom were primed for this one. This was the time, and Rhyolite was the place, to make a fortune. The boom was still resounding when the first signs of the bust appeared. Some of the smaller claims had been found wanting, and the original Bullfrog Mine had found the end of its lode.

In spite of the warning signs, Rhyolite continued to grow. The tracks of two more railroads reached town in 1907, and the population jumped from 6,000 to 10,000. Three-story buildings made of local rhyolite rock were

The Overbury Building as seen through the remains of the H. D. and L. D. Porter building. Overbury Building, originally three stories high, was equipped with a 5,000-gallon water tank on its roof.

John S. Cooke Bank of Rhyolite was built in 1908, utilizing the local white rhyolite. Building was partially destroyed in 1910 to save on taxes.

springing up. Four banks and four newspapers were in operation, and construction was started on a large, concrete schoolhouse.

Boundary lines had to be drawn in town to prevent the

Rhyolite's depot is the town's most impressive remnant. Called the finest in the state, the station served the Las Vegas and Tonopah Railroad.

encroachment of the rapidly expanding red-light district. The alley one half block east of main street was the western boundary. A new jail was built in the direction of the expansion, in order that it be handy to the customer.

The town had three separate water systems. The pressure in some mains was in excess of 70 pounds per square inch. A bad fire in the red-light district, hastened by wind, threatened to spread into the business district. The high pressure in the waterline burst the first two hoses hooked up. New hoses were strung from hydrants with lower pressure, and the blaze contained.

The financial panic of 1907 caused most of Rhyolite's mines to close down. The Montgomery Shoshone, two miles northeast of town, was a notable exception. Its continued operation prevented the immediate collapse of Rhyolite.

The Montgomery Shoshone lode was discovered by an

*Rhyolite jail was located in the middle of the red-light
district. Bars on windows were actually bars.*

Indian lad (the legend goes) who was tricked into trading it for a pair of pants and two dollars. E. A. Montgomery, the purchaser, claimed, to the contrary, that he had hired the Indian and in fact had paid him well. Further, Montgomery stated, it was by his own efforts that the best ore was located.

Montgomery sold the mine for $2 million (some report $5 million), and within a year its stock was evaluated at $7.5 million. When the mine finally closed in 1910, it had grossed $2 million in gold but was still deeply in debt on the newly built Schwab Mill.

The population of Rhyolite had been dropping for two years, but in 1910, when the Shoshone closed, it plummeted to less than a thousand. The newly completed school opened with eighteen students rattling about its spacious corridors. In 1912 the massive station of the Las Vegas and

Walls of Cooke Bank Building are silhouetted by fading evening light.

Tonopah Railroad, built just a few years earlier, was suddenly deserted when train service was terminated. A few years later the tracks were torn up for scrap, and even the diehards left town. Many homes were hauled away. All but a few of the remaining structures were burned or dynamited to save on taxes.

The railroad station was bought by the McLaughlins and remodeled as a home. It was the only major building in town to escape razing. Later the old station served as bar, gambling house, and country store. Now it is a combination residence, museum, and tourist shop. The old station stands alone amid the ravaged ruins of Rhyolite.

MAP NOTE: Details may be found on the Bullfrog, Nevada, 15 minute United States Geological Survey topographic map.

GOLD POINT, NEVADA

There are no detailed maps available for the area around Gold Point, and they are hardly necessary, since the town can be seen straight down the road from the Junction on U.S. 95 fifteen miles away. The huddle of buildings next to the light-colored mine dumps at the base of Slate Ridge is the town of Gold Point.

Seven miles of that straight road is blacktop (Nevada 3), and the remaining is good gravel. The dry, clear air fools one into thinking the town is constantly traveling away at a speed equal to one's own approach.

Of the 225 buildings that stood in the town of Gold Point (once called Lime Point and then Hornsilver) only three or four dozen remain. Compared to most ghost towns, that's a considerable remnant. There is an owner in residence at present, and he has thoughtfully laid down the ground rules by means of a small sign at the edge of town. In effect, the message asks the visitor to be careful where he trespasses and to keep hands off the property — but to take all the pictures his heart desires.

And Gold Point is photogenic. There are three "business districts," one at the deserted gas pump and store, another a few blocks northwest, and the last near a mine about a quarter of a mile to the south.

The one near the mine has on its false front a sign that can barely be made out — "Hornsilver Townsite and Telephone Company." In front of the building are the remains of the two very old gas pumps, one of them advertising filtered gasoline.

Old deserted mines are scattered in every direction. Many are quite intact. A number of gallows wheels (pulley wheels at the top of head frames) lie about as if someone were caught in the act of looting and forced to quickly divest himself of incriminating evidence.

The largest and most impressive remnant in Gold Point is the block-long business district at the northwest edge of town. In one single string there are four weathered old stores standing alone and forlorn. Three are connected and seem to gain strength from each other's presence. A two-store space separates the cluster from the end store, and beyond that are the collapsed walls of yet another place of business.

Limestone was mined here in 1868, and during that time

Gold Point's most recently occupied business district consisted of a general store and post office. The sign indicates the post office was the first to fold.

the town was called Lime Point. In 1908 high-grade silver ore was found and the town boomed. The name was changed to Hornsilver. The local newspaper was called the *Hornsilver Herald.* Thirteen saloons mushroomed, and there was talk of a railroad. By 1910 the town had reached its maximum size.

The period from 1905 to 1911 was wild. At least the old duffer from Mayer, Arizona, remembered it that way. He used to prospect the washes for gold. "Found some too," he claimed, "and I would have kept a lot more if I hadn't been cheated out of it."

He and his partner had located some good sand. They flipped to see who would go file on it. His buddy won and headed for Gold Point. He returned three days later — "with a hangover and three strangers. Seems he went and got drunk and sold our claim — *our* claim!"

The old-timer (he's the one who wanted to remain "unanimous") had little good to say about some of the merchants in the boomtowns and mining camps nearby.

"They was always cheatin' on the whiskey. Most of it was half water — wouldn't even burn your tongue." He seemed to get a little angry at something he just recalled. "There was one old crook that ran a saloon outside of Gold Point, on the way to the old Oriental camp. He used to enjoy takin' a pinch of dust for a drink, like they done years before. Everyone thought that it was all right 'til they noticed his pinchin' fingers had dents in 'em." He demonstrated with his thumb and forefinger. "Most of us guys had heard of bartenders growin' long fingernails, or runnin' their hands through the grease in their hair, but we never seen this pulled before. We raised hell with him and made him use his left hand. Then one day we see his left hand has got dents — and we find out he's been squeezin' a button in his pocket just before he takes a pinch. Told him we was gonna hang him. He didn't even take us serious, so we did. We hung him a little. Didn't hurt him much. Jest redded up his neck and maybe stretched it some."

In spite of the poor results experienced by some prospectors, increasing amounts of gold were found. Silver de-

Gold Point's earlier business district held post office, the "Hornsilver Herald" office, and thirteen saloons. Observers claimed the town "extended almost as you watched it."

posits were petering out, and by 1930 more gold was being mined than silver. Obviously the town would have to change its name again. Newly christened Gold Point, the town perked along for another twelve years before it folded. In 1955 there was one store serving the needs of thirteen residents. Now the store is closed, and the number of residents is even less.

Several of the old miners' houses have been kept up as vacation homes. Near one of them is an outhouse of unusual construction — quite appropriate to its occasional use (especially in the event of flu, the "green apple splatters," or some other similarly explosive happening) it's made entirely of ammunition boxes.

MAP NOTE: No topographic maps available.

One of a great number of deserted mines in the area southeast of Gold Point.

LIDA, NEVADA

There was gold in the Palmetto Mountains. The Indians and Mexicans mined it in the 1860s. Within a few years Americans heard about it and in the seventies moved in on the "unclaimed diggings." The settlement that grew on the site was nearly 200 miles from the nearest railroad. Silver peak, twenty miles to the north and across the mountain, was the nearest town.

Lida expanded rapidly after a road was build connecting it with Silverpeak. Machinery for two small stamp mills was hauled in and assembled at the springs near town. Much of the ore was rich — it had to be in order to balance the high cost of freighting the mill machinery at a fee of $100 per ton. Some ore was so rich it was hauled to the railhead and shipped out for processing.

When Goldfield boomed in 1904 it brought added life to Lida. The springs at the outskirts of Lida became Goldfield's water supply by means of a pipeline twenty-odd miles long. When the railroad reached Goldfield it meant

One of the finer homes in the old gold town of Lida.

lower rates on supplies for the residents of Lida. Also, low-grade ore stockpiled on the mine dumps could now be processed at a profit.

Lida grew up, and a newspaper, the *Enterprise*, came to town. The town flourished for several years then faded when many of the mines shut down during litigation. Ranching began to pay better than mining, and the nature of the community changed.

Today the town is half ghost, half ranch. Several old buildings stand vacant under massive shade trees. The old schoolhouse can be spotted by its attendant triple-door outhouse — "boys," "girls," and "teacher."

MAP NOTE: No topographic maps of the area are present available.

Small cabin is dwarfed by massive tree at the south edge of Lida.

NEVADA AREA 2

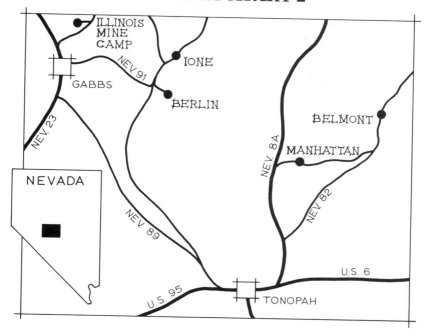

MANHATTAN, NEVADA

THE CATHOLIC CHURCH stands on a hill overlooking town. I had taken a number of low-angle shots of the old unpainted structure and had decided to climb the hill to try out the opposite view. From that direction, a few of Nevada's rare summer clouds perhaps be coerced into position. Photos completed, I wandered back past the front of the church. The steps looked inviting and there were no "No" signs in evidence. The hasp on the door was broken, apparently smashed. I reached for the handle, and as my hand touched metal a shot rang out. My hand jerked back instantly. I took inventory, then looked about. Someone had determined that a shot fired in the air, at a precisely timed moment, would serve as an effective deterrent. That someone had no doubt pulled the stunt on others. He probably keeps a good eye out, fearful he will miss another chance at a little fun. I got the message, and I understood the necessity of his delivering it. Some visitors leave with mementos more substantial than exposed film.

Manhattan has had an on-again, off-again history. Silver found here in 1866 resulted in the construction of a mill, but it failed to show a profit and was abandoned three years later. In 1905 some cattlemen spotted an outcrop of "jewelry quality" ore. They claimed it and named it for the date of discovery — April Fool. That summer eight townsites were laid out in the vicinity, and the usual competition between landmen ensued. Mine speculators moved in the next year and spread exaggerations all over Nevada. Soon 4,000 people had rushed to the spot, most of them from Tonopah, Fifty miles south. The road was constantly filled with rigs and autos, one every half mile or so. The dust never settled.

Lots in town were expensive, and store owners built on their entire lot, attaching each new building to the sidewall of the last. One lucky merchant bought a 30-foot space between two stores and simply raised a front, a back, and a roof. Fire hazards due to this kind of construction were

Catholic Church was moved in from deserted Belmont. The church fell into disuse a second time when Manhattan also became deserted.

Manhattan's Main Street was once a solid string of connected buildings. Structure at left was adapted for use as firehouse.

ignored. The topographic map of the vicinity shows a solid bar on each side of the road, indicating long strings of connected buildings. The town had its own electric power plant, three banks, two newspapers, a number of stores, and plenty of "water holes."

The quake hit San Francisco the following year, and Manhattan's financial supporters went home (with their money) to repair damage to their holdings. Manhattan collapsed, but new placer strikes brought it back to life two years later. A particularly rich float was found east of town at the White Caps(s) Mine. A mill was built, and the population of Manhattan stabilized at nearly one thousand.

The town had nearly died for the second time by 1939, when dredging offered a new flicker of life. When that effort ceased in 1947, the town died its most recent death. It's due to come back to life again any time — it always has.

Meanwhile it's a delightful ghost town. An old rock building at the east end of town has a weathered sign over its door that reads "post office," but showing through are the

The finest homes in Manhattan once lined the street on hill just south of town. A few of the homes are now used as summer retreats.

Mine shack and head frame are just a few steps east of Manhattan's deserted post office.

letters "B A N K." Just a few steps away are the hoist works shed and gallows frame of a small mine. The Toiyabe Hall stands across the street, two-storied and impressive. Strung along the main street are an old meat market, five houses, and a general store. The many gaps along the once-solid string of storefronts were created when a number of merchants moved their places of business to a booming placer camp on Round Mountain. When they removed their stores, they took the outside walls of adjacent buildings with them. Most gaps are at least three stores wide.

The little general store is the only place doing business now. Recent "progress" has been almost too much for the gas pump. Its rate adjustment won't reach the current 50- to 60-cent price of gas. It still reads 30 cents per gallon, but a sign on the pump tells the customer to fill up, then just double the total.

MAP NOTE: Excellent detail is displayed on the 1914 Manhattan and Vicinity, Nevada, 3"-to-the-mile United States Geological Survey topographic map. Sadly, the map is now out of print and cannot be purchased. Some libraries in Nevada have the map and will permit copies to be made.

Parts of a small stamp mill that once processed ore near the Mount Moriah Cemetery, a mile or so west of Manhattan.

BELMONT, NEVADA

It can only be described as an oasis. In the middle of town, surrounded by large shade trees, a spring bubbles forth, its steady flow giving rise to a small stream that wanders south through town. Within a mile the waters of the stream are sapped and then swallowed by the thirsty desert sand.

Belmont enjoys ideal weather during most of the year, due mainly to the 7,000-foot elevation. There are times, however, when heavy winds dominate life in town. Guy wires to the west and south of many buildings attest to the strength of the winds. Heavy winter snows (seven feet in four days on one occasion) can pile up and cut the town off from civilization for weeks at a time.

West side of Belmont's main thoroughfare held a general store (right), undertaker's parlor, and Mrs. Hughes' Boardinghouse.

Rose Walter is the ranking old-timer, and the venerable first lady of Belmont. Rose and her housekeeper-companion live in a large, well-kept rock home at the north end of town. These two ladies, and the couple that own the newly opened gas station-bar-cafe at the opposite end of town, make up the complete roster of year-around residents.

Strung out along the main street of town are a number of impressive remains of the once-notable town. Across the stream are more buildings. Dominating that side of town is the grand old Nye County Courthouse. Two-story brick, with tall wooden cupola and numerous chimneys, the structure was, and still is, the fanciest building in the county. It was here that the "town character" held sway as district attorney. Elected as a joke, he took his job seri-

Rear view of buildings on east side of Main Street shows impressive rock work.

Cosmopolitan Music Hall once hosted the famous Fay Templeton.

ously — so seriously that he refused to leave office at the end of the term. The newly elected D.A. tried to assume office, but Old Andy held out for nine days, sleeping in the courthouse office and having meals sent in.

Silver, found in 1865, resulted in an immediate influx of fortune seekers. With assays at more than $100 per ton and over a thousand tons of ore blocked out, there was little reason to believe Belmont would be a town to go bust quickly. Merchants built with a justifiable hope of permanence, and within two years the population had reached 6,000. When Belmont secured the county seat, plans were laid to build a prideful courthouse. Clay deposits were located four miles west of town, and a brick factory was constructed. From that brick the courthouse was built, and from that edifice emanated an aura that inspired confidence in those who would build other durable structures. Belmont grew to 10,000 and boasted two newspapers, an oyster house, and a music hall. Society made the news, but

Buckled and leaning, wooden structures at south end of Belmont
will soon be reduced to foundations and rubble.

rougher elements were making the headlines. Two union
organizers were chased out of town. When they were found
hiding out nearby, they were hauled in and hung!

Irish laborers in 1867 confronted Boss Canfield and ac-
cused him of hiring Cornishmen at lower wages to replace
the Irish. Tempers heated, and soon Canfield was being
toted about town on a rail. When a former lawman, Louis
Bodrow, tried to slow things down, shots rang out and two
men fell to the ground. Bodrow and Pat Dignon lay dead.
Bodrow had been shot sixteen times and then stabbed
repeatedly. He got off two shots before he expired, and
Dignon intercepted one of them.

During some of Belmont's more lawless years, a vigilante group maintained order by staging occasional hang-

Old cowboys never die. They just pull their rigs off the road.

*Impressive ruins of the combination mill are just east of Belmont.
A second, more modern, mill, also deserted, is
half a mile to the south.*

*Nye County Courthouse, built in 1867, had numerous chimneys
serving heaters in every office. Note the late-
model horse trailer in foreground.*

ings. Generally the job was done on the sly, to avoid in-crimination, but each time, a sign bearing the number "301" was attached to the victim. The lesson was clear and effective. A few more crooks slipped out of town each time word spread that the "301" was forming up for an evening's chores.

By 1885 $15 million in silver had been taken from the hills. Mines produced until the late thirties then abruptly shut down. With the shutdown, payrolls stopped. Stores closed for lack of customers, and the town became sud-denly quiet. The Catholic Church was moved to Manhat-tan, there to become deserted once again. In 1903 only thirty-six people registered to vote in Belmont.

But the town isn't altogether dead. The little saloon at the south end of town is open. Travelers can obtain suste-nance and libation. One can even buy gasoline; however, the procedure is a bit unusual.

First you borrow the pump handle from the bartender, then pump the gas into a glass cylinder atop the pump. The gasoline then flows by gravity through the nozzle and into the gas tank of the car. You check the pump handle back in when you pay the bartender for the gas. Now that's progress!

MAP NOTE: No topographic map of the area is presently available.

IONE, NEVADA

West of Tonopah, dust devils trace their serpentine paths across the dry flats, gathering substance as finely powdered earth is blown high in an ever-tightening spiral. Heavier spheres of tumbleweed ride low, bouncing along, nearly escaping, then swinging violently inward to orbit in tight circles. At times a dozen or more of the dry tumbleweeds are carried crazily along, like ponies on a merry-go-round gone wild.

Passing through one of the larger whirlwinds is an experience. First the wind and debris batter one side of the observer. Then, after the passage of a miniscule eye, the opposite side is delivered an equal blow. The passage is quick and harmless to all but the very delicate. Butterflies, Kleenex, newspapers, even handkerchiefs "out of the hand" are occasionally carried to extreme heights, to fall back gently when the centripetal grip is relaxed.

North and west of Tonopah, past the playground of the

View of Ione from the Shamrock Canyon Road shows the extent of old town and the influx of a new breed of trailer-towing prospectors.

*Trappings of the mining trade hang all about this small rock structure at
the east end of Ione. Bars, made of ore car rails, are too
widely spaced to serve any worthwhile purpose.*

dust devils and a dozen or so miles east of Gabbs, a narrow
canyon in the Shoshone Mountains cradles the remains of
the old mining town of Ione.

In 1863 silver was found in Ione Canyon to the northeast,
and a camp grew on the site. The narrow canyon offered
little room to expand, so the town was moved downstream
to the flats at the canyon mouth. Ione became the first
county seat of Nye County in 1864, and the town soon
exceeded 500 in population. Several mills were built, but
the ore in the region never lived up to the mill's capacities,
let alone the promoter's expectations. In 1867 the county
seat was moved to Belmont. In spite of the recent extrac-

Old "hot head" engine remains at the Shamrock
Mine, half a mile southeast of Ione.

tion of mercury, less than a million dollars in precious
metals has been taken from the region.

A number of old mines are strung out along the four-mile
length of Shamrock Canyon just east of Ione. One of them,
the Shamrock Mine perched on the north slope, is accessible by a recently improved road. At the mine site, an old
"hot head" steam engine still sits on its pads, apparently in
running order. The shed giving it protection is shorn of its
roofing, and cracks between boards let in narrow bands of
light, contouring the shapes of the machine within.

At the west end of town, a low rock structure dominates a

*Walls of this once-fancy home at the west end of Ione are
more than two feet thick. Fireplace in rear
end wall is flush inside and out.*

rise on the north side of the road. Its walls are more than
two feet thick. The east wall contains a flush fireplace. Not
flush just on the inside but also on the outer surface. With
the super-thick walls, the fireplace is merely a hollow portion hidden in the middle. A beam along the ridge supports
rough-sawn two-by-fours that measure an actual 2¼ by
3½ inches. These are apparently the ancestors of the present 1½-by-3¼-inch anemic offsprings. Over the rafters,
waste slabwood was nailed on, then bark was laid on the
boards, and the whole covered with dirt and a crop of grass
planted.

While it was occupied the owner kept the grass watered.
The shade kept the dirt cool and the house comfortable.
When the last occupant moved out, the roof died.

MAP NOTE: The 15 minute Ione, Nevada, United States Geological Survey map is an excellent aid in exploring the area. A series of Xs, indicating
prospect holes, surround Ione on three sides. Many tunnels and shafts
are indicated, sprinkled along the two canyons leading northeast and
southeast from town.

BERLIN, NEVADA

Two hundred million years ago, sixty-foot monsters swam in the shallow seas that covered most of the western states. Warm-blooded, mammalian, and shaped somewhat like a lizard, the ichthyosaur lived, propagated, and died in much the same manner as the whales of the present era. The bodies of some ichthyosaurs sank in the deep ooze present in some shallows. In time the ooze hardened to become a mold of the animal's skeleton. Slowly, water made acidic with carbon dioxide dissolved the bones.

Much later the area was covered with volcanic matter. Over an extended period of time, rainwater laden with minerals filtered through the overburden and filled the bone cavities, recreating the skeletons in agate and other precipitated rock.

Fossils of the ancient animals were found in 1860, thirty-five years before silver was discovered. In 1898,

Berlin, smog-free and uncongested.

Old thirty-stamp mill of Berlin stands at the interface of Ione Valley and the Shoshone Mountains.

three years after the silver strike, many of the claims were bought up by the Nevada Company (a New York outfit) and a mill constructed. The small town of Berlin grew around the mill. The population held at about 200 for ten years, then dropped to a handful in 1909 when the mill shut down.

The buildings of Berlin have changed little from the time it became deserted. Some of the pot-bellied stoves have disappeared, and the metal has been salvaged from the mill. Prospectors have occasionally used cabins in town as a base of operations. Presently, one of the old cabins is occupied by a Nevada State Parks employee. The town is used as an entrance gate to Ichthyosaur State Park.

MAP NOTE: The 15 minute Ione, Nevada, United States Geological Survey map shows the site of Berlin but oddly fails to pinpoint the location or extent of the fossil beds.

ILLINOIS MINE CAMP, NEVADA

The Paradise Peak topographic map is littered with evidence of old towns and mining camps. Ellsworth, Craig Station, and Downeyville are shown and labeled as sites. Paradise Peak Mine Camp, Sierra Magnesite Mine Camp, and Brucite are depicted by numerous black squares, indicating present occupation. The date on the map is 1948, and it would be logical to assume that at least one of the last three towns would by now be a deserted camp worthy of inspection. At the north end of the map, the Big Chief Mine, the Victory Tungsten Mine, and the Illinois Mine Camp are shown. It seemed likely that one of these sites might also prove to be a little-known town or camp, rarely visited and virgin of any publicity.

At Ellsworth and Craig, remains were sparse. At Downeyville I could find only mine shafts. The Victory Tungsten Mine Camp was small and in intermittent use. The Sierra Magnesite Camp, right next to Gabbs, consisted only of concrete slabs. Brucite was now a part of the excavation of the huge mine operation being carried out a mile east of Gabbs. Gabbs, the biggest town within fifty miles, was a very small community with only one cafe, but it hardly qualified as a ghost town.

At one time, a town called Lodi existed about ten miles northeast of Gabbs. It had a population of 100 and was the supply point for the Illinois Mine Camp two miles to the west. The map showed no town by the name of Lodi, but it did show a tank (small water reservoir) by that name. I expected to find the slate wiped equally clean at the Illinois Mine Camp but was pleasantly surprised to find a number of impressive remnants. Finally! After a dozen disappointments, here was a site worth a few rolls of film and an afternoon's "exploration."

Deciphering the remains of deserted sites involves a lot of inspection, some deduction, a share of guesswork, and a residue of mystery. A ghost town hunter quickly becomes a speculative historian.

Beside the road at the mine camp stood a small, rock-walled, sod-roofed building with a wooden vent rising at the back. The fixtures were not that of an outhouse, so the logical assumption (there were shelves on the sides) was that the building served as a powder house. It would naturally have a stout door and lock, but these were miss-

*When the Illinois Mine was in operation, boiler at right supplied steam
to hoist engine mounted on concrete pad to left of head frame.
Ore was chuted into the shed for sorting.*

ing. A bit further along the little-used road, a deep mine
shaft required careful avoidance. Ordinary passage put
the pickup wheels within a foot of the lip. There was little
to worry about, however, as the truck was larger than the
shaft. However, when approaching on foot the prudent
observer would maintain his distance, since the lip slopes
in and is covered with small, rounded rocks ready to ease
one's entrance.

Large-diameter metal hoops told of wooden tanks that
once stood here — probably a cyanide unit for extracting
stubborn gold. Perhaps tailings were reworked for gold
missed on the first attempt.

Two corrugated steel tanks lay crumpled in the gully.
They appeared to be either blown up by dynamite or blown
down by wind — probably the latter, since the remains
were more battered than bulged.

Rock mill foundations occupied the slope near the banks

of the gully. The absence of further remains would indicate that the steel was removed — perhaps the entire mill. Then again, this could be one of those structures sacrificed in the making of a B-grade western movie.

A sign in the center of town marks the spot as the route of an emergency stock driveway. Amazing — it makes one wonder how many head of stock may have ended up at shaft bottoms.

Down the hill and east a few hundred yards, past a number of jackstrawed woodpiles (probably living quarters), was a stout brick cubical in the midst of extensive brick rubble. It must have been a bank vault at the company offices. Nearby was a square concrete foundation, very stout for its size. A mystery. A few steps to the east the ground sounded hollow. Yet car tracks indicated it was safe to traverse. A bit more to the east, a tall, broad vertical expanse of brick provided the answer. Doors in the face led to underground tunnellike chambers of the type used to smelt ore. The tunnels led to the square concrete found-

Metal tanks were either blown up or blown down. Bases for the tanks can be seen at upper right.

Small smelter, built in 1878, proved the local ore to be of sufficient value to warrant construction of larger smelter seen in background.

ation, which now quite clearly was a chimney base. A short distance away was a small rock kiln or smelter. It was the obvious forerunner. Both structures had the same angled brackets to hold the removable doors. None of the doors was at hand. They would have been metal doors and therefore would have been sold for scrap during one of the past wars.

Facts concerning the camp are few. Residents of Gabbs were able to provide some, and a few paragraphs referring to the town were gleaned from the Nevada State Archives.

Gold found here in 1874 resulted in a small smelter (the one built of rock?) being constructed nearby. The camp that grew about the mine and smelter included a store, saloon, boarding house (perhaps that explains the long, narrow foundation below the mine), and a population of several hundred.

The mine was closed and reopened a number of times.

Each time the camp received a new name: Marble and Bob were used, and some claim the camp was called Lodi for a time. However, about 1908 the real Lodi was laid out at the site of the present Lodi tanks, and the mine camp then went under the name of Illinois.

Things really got going about 1910, when Lodi began to look like a town and new veins were located at the Illinois Mine. A large smelter was built (the brick one). Severe flooding in the shaft brought things to a halt about the time of World War I. Just before World War II, a last effort was made (the corrugated tanks) to extract the remaining ore.

Except for the small concrete water tank there is nothing to mark the site of Lodi, but the remains at Illinois Mine Camp (or Marble, or Bob) are as numerous and varied as the names the camp has carried.

MAP NOTE: The Paradise Peak, Nevada, 15 minute United States Geological Survey topographic map shows a wealth of old sites.

NEVADA AREA 3

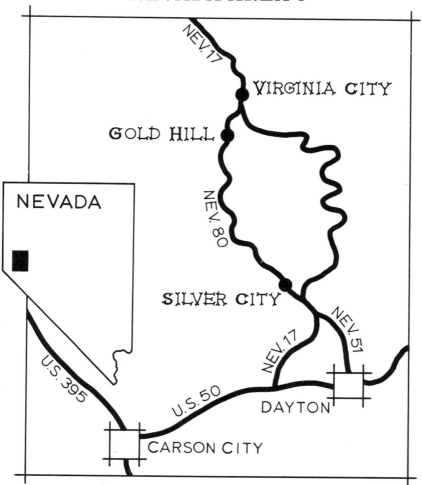

VIRGINIA CITY, NEVADA

THE OLD PROSPECTOR was halfway into tying on a good one. Old Virginny, he was called, probably because, drunk or sober, he was continually rattling on about his home state. He had just bought a fresh bottle and was headed toward camp by way of the straightest line possible when he stumbled on the rough ground and fell forward, bottle-arm outstretched. Unfortunately there was a rock at the point of contact. The whiskey flooded out of the shattered glass and soaked quickly into the ground. Not one to waste a full bottle, the old prospector gathered himself up and proclaimed, "I christen this ground Virginia."

If it hadn't been for that rock at the end of Old Virginny's sprawl, the town might have kept its original name — Silver City. As it was, the story was told so many times that the christening was accepted. After all, it was reasoned, anyone who could think that fast deserved the right to name the town!

The story of Virginia City started ten years back, when the barren ground was called Gold Canyon. Some folk passing through to California had panned a little gold in the canyon prior to 1850, but it was silver that Allen and Hosea Grosch found a few years later. They quietly ground the blue quartz and smelted it down in their small assay furnace. Henry Comstock, called Old Pancake, prospecting in the canyon at the time, noticed all the secrecy going on and

Piper's Opera House, the Knights of Pythias, Schoenfeld's Furniture, and the Miners' Union Hall stand in a row, one block off the main street of Virginia City.

St. Mary's in the Mountains, built in 1877, over shadows St. Paul's Espiscopal Church on the downside of Virginia City.

knew that the two men had made a strike. He searched and watched but never figured out where the Grosches were getting their ore. He wasn't even sure whether it was silver or gold ore that the two brothers worked on in such secrecy.

Word slowly leaked out that gold and/or silver had been found, and soon the hills were dotted with pick and shovel men. O'Riley and McLaughlin arrived late and quickly staked their claims at the fringe, before those were taken by the next batch of arrivals. Later they worked it over thoroughly and uncovered a gold-bearing quartz ledge. Old Pancake Comstock, as was his habit, immediately claimed prior filing. To humor him, O'Riley and McLaughlin took him in on the deal. The find was the first tap on what was to be called the Comstock Lode.

The ore was dirty and difficult to work. After crushing and panning the wash for gold, the discolored remains were quickly thrown away. One prospector, familiar with silver, quietly picked up some of the leavings and had them assayed. The discarded waste ran over $4,000 per ton of silver — more than the value per ton of gold already extracted!

Word of the new find brought a second flow of prospectors. During the spring of 1860 nearly two hundred a day were entering the Washoe area. According to one reporter, promoters outnumbered the prospectors fifty to one. The same reporter gave detailed accounts of the terrain and the weather. He claimed that heavy snow, prolonged runoffs, and a vicious wind called the Washoe Zephyr made the place "essentially infernal in every respect!"

It wasn't yet known that a heavy body of ore lay under Davidson Mountain, running parallel to the canyon floor

Old Fourth Ward School had four stories and fancy arches over the windows – but no fire escape.

Once-bustling Main Street of Virginia City still bustles, especially on weekends. Town once boasted 100 saloons and a yearly consumption of 75,000 gallons of hard liquor.

and the streets of the burgeoning town. The extent of the ore would be only partly determined during the boom of the sixties, when half a million a month would be mined. In two years that lode would expire and the town would be deserted.

Then, eight years later, a group of investors with imagination and foresite would investigate and catalog the full extent of the lode. In the process, the main lode, the big one underneath, would be found and the real boom would ensue. It would last eight years.

Samuel Langhorne Clemens, his river piloting job interupted by the Civil War, had wandered west to find a new job. The papers were full of promises and exaggerations concerning the big Washoe strike. Four thousand claims had been filed in the single year of 1860. Clemens joined with three others suffering from the same fever and set out for Virginia City.

The area was touted as the "richest mineral region on God's footstool," but Clemens soon found out that $4,000

*Delightful old piano player provides honky-tonk music
in one of Virginia City's better beer joints.*

per ton in the papers was more like $400 per ton on the
ledger. Clemens, with his three partners, a blacksmith and
two lawyers, filed a claim near the Humboldt Mining
Camp. They named it the Monarch of the Mountains and
proceeded to dig away at the quartz. Digging and blasting
proved to be a difficult way to get rich. Clemens "resigned"
several times. When the shaft reached a depth of twelve
feet, the partners collected a few of the best samples and
headed for Virginia City to do a little promoting. Within
days the four had traded for shares in fifty different mines,

*Engine 27 of the Virginia and Truckee Railroad stands
idle on a short piece of track in Virginia City.*

all highly touted but probably inferior to the twelve-foot hole they had just left.

Clemens took a job as a reporter with the *Territorial Enterprise* for $25 per week. He filled a vacancy created when William Wright (who wrote under the name of Dan deQuille) left town at the suggestion of an irate reader.

Wright was one of the greatest liars of all time. When there was no news he created some, and his creations were classic. One of his best concerned an individual who had invented a type of vest or armor designed to let the desert traveler remain cool even in the middle of summer at the bottom of the hottest desert wash. The vest was actually a large thin sponge, Wright wrote, with a water reservoir at the back and a rubber bulb under the arm to act as a pump. A squeeze on the bulb, and water saturated the vest. Evaporation of the water cooled the wearer. The inventor, according to Wright's news release, headed into Death Valley on a test cruise. A few days later a prospector hurried into a nearby camp asking for help to go rescue the crazy inventor. It seems the vest worked too well, and he was found sitting in the noon day sun, frozen stiff, with a foot-long icicle dangling from his chin!

Clemens learned a few lessons from Wright. He learned to lie with authority and to do it under an assumed name. At the paper, he signed his work Josh. Later, in 1863, he began using the name that brought him fame — Mark Twain.

Virginia City had two disastrous fires. Each time the town rebuilt even finer than before, but each time the fire seemed to signal an impending bust.

The fire of '63 caused a loss of nearly $10 million. A fire tower was built on the mountain to spot the first smoke of the next disaster. Two years after the town was rebuilt, the first lode ran out and the town shrank from 15,000 to 6,000.

Location of the big lode brought prosperity again in 1873. Silver was extracted at a phenomenal rate — about $1 million a week. A mint was built in Carson city to handle the gold and silver. The town had five breweries making 75,000 gallons of hard stuff each year, and well over one hundred saloons were kept busy distributing the supply. Below town, 750 miles of tunnels pursued the huge lode. There was $900 million dollars worth of ore in that lode. When the end was found, Virginia City collapsed. That happened just two years after the second big fire.

Much of the Virginia and Truckee line from Carson City to Virginia City was either high trestle or deep rocky cut. Note people standing on walkway below tracks.

There had been signs of failure for several years. Many of the shafts were flooding with hot water. High temperatures made for short working times and great expense. A gentleman named Adolph Sutro proposed a four-mile tunnel from the lode under Virginia City to the flats southeast of town. He received little encouragement. Mine owners could see the end of the lode but weren't about to admit it. Sutro built the tunnel and ended up the owner of many of the dewatered mines. It is doubtful that the ore made available was enough to pay the expense of the tunnel.

By 1881 the population of Virginia City was less than 400. That's about what it is now, on a miserable day in the middle of the winter. In the summer, crowds of tourists fill the streets. It's still a boom-and-bust situation in Virginia City.

MAP NOTE: The Virginia City, Nevada, 15 minute United States Geological Survey topographic map is an excellent source of detailed information.

GOLD HILL, NEVADA

Before it flooded, the Yellow Jacket Mine at Gold Hill, Nevada, was the biggest producer on the south end of the Comstock Lode. When a blast of dynamite opened a passage to a hot spring, the tunnels flooded with 170-degree water. Miners could work only a few minutes at a time in the hot, humid atmosphere near the water. Rest periods were longer than the work shifts. Even allocations of 100 pounds of ice per man per day were not enough to entice men to stay on the job.

Eventually the Sutro Tunnel was built and a south lateral connected with the East Yellow Jacket workings. The mine became workable again, but within a short time the lode was exhausted. While it lasted, the Yellow Jacket had poured large payrolls into the life stream of Gold Hill.

Back in 1869, tent towns were strung along the length of Gold Canyon from the narrows called Devil's Gate at the

The Gold Hill Hotel was built on the site of the first recorded claim in town. It also had the distinction of being the first hotel in Nevada.

Massive head frame of the Yellow Jacket Mine stands on Gold Hill's Main Street. Mine tapped gold and silver from the south end of the Comstock Lode.

south, on up to side canyons appropriately labeled Six Mile and Seven Mile. As tunnels located the lodes, the towns consolidated. Virginia City and Gold Hill occupied sites on either side of a low hump in the middle of the canyon.

Both towns graduated from tent towns to rock and mud and, finally, to frame and brick. When the big lode was worked, both towns had large numbers of pretentious structures. Rivalry was great. At one time Virginia City attempted to annex Gold Hill. Gold Hill retaliated by attempting to split the county into two chunks and thereby become a county seat equal in status to Virginia City. The effort failed, since it was thought ridiculous to have two county seats within a mile of each other.

It appeared, in 1864, that the ore had run out. Things quieted down, and population along the canyon dwindled,

Beer wagon once hauled barrels of beer from the brewery in background.
Many buildings in Gold Hill have been renovated by their
owners to be used as residences or summer homes.

but Gold Hill continued to survive, due in part to its location on the main supply route to Virginia City. When the big lode was found, both towns boomed bigger than ever. Gold Hill zoomed to nearly 10,000 and bragged of street lamps and three fire companies.

*Freight wagon is one of many wagons sprinkled about Gold Hill.
Residents are restoring a variety of horse-drawn vehicles.*

The ore ran out for the second time in 1878, and in rapid order most of the population left for other parts. Saloons shut down, and the *Gold Hill News* ceased publication.

When the post office closed down in 1943, there were less than a dozen people left in town. Lately some of the old buildings have been converted to residences. Their exteriors have been restored to appear as they did one hundred years ago. The brewery and old hotel are excellent examples. The town is loaded with old wagons. Beer wagons, freight wagons, buggies, and stagecoaches are found sprinkled about, the proud possessions of history-minded citizens bent on reconditioning them for display.

MAP NOTE: The Virginia City, Nevada, 15 minute United States Geological Survey topographic map shows the town, the Sutro Tunnel, and a number of the sites of small satellite towns.

NEVADA AREA 4

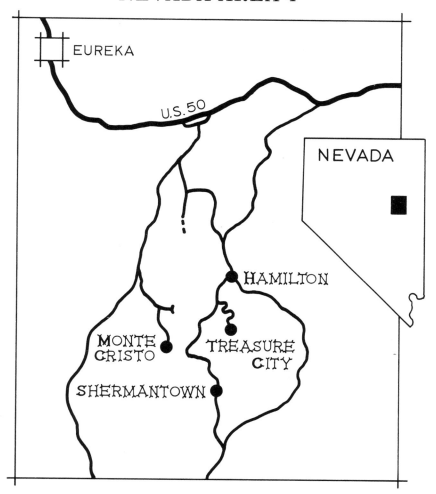

EUREKA

U.S. 50

NEVADA

HAMILTON

MONTE CRISTO

TREASURE CITY

SHERMANTOWN

MONTE CRISTO, NEVADA

IT TAKES FOUR MAPS to understand the lay of the land and to pinpoint items of interest in the White Pine Mountains of Humbolt National Forest in east central Nevada. Within a radius of five miles around the juncture of these maps are enough old town sites, mine ruins, and mill remains to keep a back-road explorer busy for a week. Roads alternately follow dry canyons and skirt mountains, joining to form a spectacular three-dimensional network.

The road into Monte Cristo crosses deposits of soft rock that powders easily to a flour-fine consistency. In places the ruts are a foot deep in the nearly fluid residue. White rooster tails follow each vehicle, and hang suspended long after their passage.

Monte Cristo lies at the western edge of the Humbolt Mountains, on the sloping foothills immediately below 10,745-foot Mount Hamilton. The Monte Cristo Spring is a quarter of a mile to the east. A mile to the north, the Silver Bell Mine hangs in a steep side canyon. To the southeast an unnamed tunnel bores into the west shoulder of Pogonip Ridge.

Monte Cristo was the first camp in the White Pine District. Established in 1865, it served as a mill town for the

Interior of rock building in Monte Cristo shows repeated efforts to brace roof against collapse.

Local sedimentary rock laid up by experts resulted in corners that have remained plumb for more than 180 years.

west-slope mines. The ore paid out at less than $100 a ton — hardly enough to spawn a rush. For three years the little five-stamp mill pounded away at the stingy ore. Then the whole area seemed to explode as 50,000 prospectors stormed into the White Pine Mountains.

It started when a hungry Shoshone Indian traded some silver-bearing rock for a plate of beans. The Indian eventually guided A. J. Leathers, Tom Murphy, and Ed Marchand to the deposit on the far side of a knob that was subsequently named Treasure Hill. The claim staked out was termed the Hidden Treasure. Old Napais Jim had accepted a plate of beans in trade for a vein that would later be valued at half a million dollars.

The rush brought some business to Monte Cristo, but the big action was in other parts of the White Pine Mountains. The town continued to suffer along on the same inferior ore. After the excitement passed, Monte Cristo was still there. It even expanded with a new mill to handle some better ore being dug fifteen miles to the west. By 1890, even the mediocre ore deposits were expended, and the town became deserted.

Now there is left only a brick smokestack, numerous foundations, some rock walls, and a sod-roofed structure about to collapse.

Nearby, the cycle is about to repeat, as tents and trailers are pitched on the site of a "new strike." Freshly planted signs delineate the claim and express the hopes of the new developers of the "Marjory Lode."

MAP NOTE: Necessary for a proper guide to the area are the Illipah, Pancake Summit, Green Springs, and Treasure Hill, Nevada, 15 minute United States Geological Survey topographic maps.

Smelters at Monte Cristo began operating in 1866, two years before the big strike at Treasure Hill, several miles to the east. Smelter processed low-grade local ore, never tasting the silver-bearing rock of the big strike, due to inter-vening mountainous terrain.

HAMILTON, NEVADA

If the Shoshone Indian Napias Jim had known that his mountains would be overrun by 50,000 white men, he would have gone hungry rather than trade his silver find for that plate of beans.

After Murphy, Leathers, and Marchand claimed the Hidden Treasure Mine in 1868, a boom took place that resulted in the construction of a dozen towns, four of which would exceed 5,000 souls. The ground would be torn up, roads built, and the local rock reassembled in the form of large multistoried places of business. Five years later these same empire builders would abruptly leave. Evidence of their efforts, the large rock buildings, would endure somewhat longer.

Two settlements grew quickly around the first discoveries during the spring of 1860 — one on top of Treasure Hill, the other on its north slope three miles away. For a

Hamilton's business district held 101 saloons and fifty stores doing general business. The double wall formed by adjacent buildings has managed to survive.

few months the two communities were considered to be the same town and were referred to as White Pine, the name given to the newly created mining district.

Within six months the towns had developed separate identities. On the hill was Treasure City. Down below, enjoying a better climate and a dependable water supply, was the town of Hamilton.

Hamilton quickly became a promoter's dream. Stocks were bought and sold over half a dozen counters. Fortunes were made overnight, and some were lost even quicker.

Arch of unknown building at north end of town demonstrates a quality of workmanship that proved unnecessary. Hamilton was deserted five years after it was incorporated.

*Storm clouds gather above Treasure Hill before descending
on the remnants of Hamilton's residential district.*

Residential lots sold for a flat $5,000. A corner lot on main
street went for $25,000.

The first Fourth of July celebrated in the White Pine
District was a combined effort of the competing towns of
Treasure City and Hamilton. One town handled the
parade, the other the debates and speeches. A huge
American flag was sewed up, utilizing scrap materials.
The blue portion was cut from a scarf bought from a Mor-
mon family passing through. A few days later, when a
financial wheel came to town, the flag served a second
purpose. The financier's money was badly needed, and
when he demanded sheets for his straw tick in the local
hotel, the flag was torn in half and sacrificed. The investor
didn't realize how lucky he was. Just a few weeks before,
the town didn't have even a hotel, and the one building
then in existence (a saloon) was busy 24 hours a day.

Within one year of the strike on Treasure Hill, Hamilton
had 10,000 residents, a school, a debating club, and half the
Jezebels in Nevada. Miners were living in caves, rock and
mud huts — even barrels laid end-to-end. The town was
designated as the county seat of newly formed White Pine

County, and in two months a $55,000 courthouse blossomed. The business district was several blocks long, filled both sides of the street, and contained a number of two-story buildings.

The rush to Hamilton was wilder and faster during 1869 than any gold or silver boom in history. It seemed that everyone who had missed out on the Comstock was at Hamilton, determined to get in on the ground floor.

When a gun fight broke out between two gamblers, one correspondent from a big city newspaper reported that shots were exchanged all over town, and "unfortunately neither one was shot, but an innocent horse was killed."

The vault, a tall corner, and large basement are all that is left of the Withington Hotel, one of Hamilton's finest.

Nearly two hundred mining companies sent their bullion out to the railhead at Elko, 140 miles away. Robberies averaged more than one a week.

The *Daily Inland Empire* published reports of every new find, and that fall a subdivision was laid out to handle the influx of new citizens. The population hit 15,000 before winter set in. With winter came the cold realization that the silver deposits were shallow and soon would be depleted. Mining stocks became difficult to unload. Companies folded, and construction halted in the town of Hamilton.

By spring half the citizens of Hamilton had moved out. An amazing number of fires broke out in the business district. A cigar store owner was caught after setting fire to his well-insured establishment. He might have escaped a seven-year prison term if he hadn't been spotted shutting the valve of the water supply. As a result of this fire, one-third of the town was destroyed.

The town is now completely deserted. Only rock walls, some partially collapsed brick structures, a group of frame homes, and a few sod-roof shanties mark the site. There hasn't been a fire on main street for almost 100 years.

MAP NOTE: Necessary for a proper guide to the area are the Illipah, Pancake Summit, Green Springs, and Treasure Hill, Nevada, 15 minute United States Geological Survey topographic maps.

TREASURE CITY, NEVADA

Wells Fargo had an office in Treasure City and another office three miles down the slope of Treasure Hill at the town of Hamilton. Each day the stage brought mail to Hamilton, and riders raced up the three-mile stretch to Treasure City. Bets were placed daily, and when a second competing line built offices in both towns the competition

Many of Treasure City's buildings were several stories high at the down-hill end. Walls were laid up with sparing use of mortar.

Treasure City's main thoroughfare jogs occasionally to miss open shafts. Pogonip Ridge is in right background, with Pancake Range in the distance.

became fierce. Claims, mines, and entire fortunes were wagered on the mail races.

A walk through the deserted town today yields a thrill of a different sort. Open shafts are everywhere. In some places the main street through town has to make a quick jog to miss a shaft. Remnants of rock buildings stretch for a quarter of a mile under the brow of Treasure Hill. In the center of town, a rock wall was built to hold mine waste from rolling down on the main street.

Judging from the remains, some of the business buildings were two stories high in front and three stories at the rear. Some of the rocks used in construction measured more than two feet on a side. There are remains of more than two dozen such buildings along the west side of the street. All are roofless. Many are merely stubborn corners and partly crumbled walls.

Records indicate that during the two-year period of 1869 and '70, forty-two business establishments were built and the population passed the 6,000 mark.

The weather on top of Treasure Hill was abominable. The winters were windy and cold. When the wind slacked, a stinging fog called the "pogonip" set in over the city. It may have been the first case of inversion smog recorded in the state.

For a time Treasure City threatened to outshine Hamilton. Hamilton had the county seat, but Treasure City had the largest stock exchange, and seats sold for $300. It had fewer saloons than its neighbor down the hill, but it boasted a larger business district.

More than 13,000 claims were filed in the vicinity of town. Much of the $20 million in silver taken in the White Pine District came from these mines. The deposits were shallow, easily reached, and quickly depleted.

When the silver began to run out in 1870, a few mines remained operating, but even those could see the end of their holdings. The big fire of 1874 wiped out most of the frame portion of town. By 1880 only fourteen people registered to vote. The place has been deserted for the last eighty years. The smog problem has finally been licked.

MAP NOTE: The Illipah, Pancake Summit, Green Springs, and Treasure Hill, Nevada, 15 minute United States Geological Survey maps are a proper guide to this area.

Old structure on mine dump above Treasure City appears to have served as drive shaft or cable pylon.

SHERMANTOWN, NEVADA

The sagebrush is eight feet tall, and it grows all over the flats. The remains of Shermantown stand above the sage in a few places but in the main are hidden beneath heavy growth.

Of all the towns in the White Pine District, Shermantown had the most desirable location. Water was plentiful, the soil was good, and the valley was protected. It was

Building in Shermantown are nearly buried in heavy growth. Walls of second building can barely be made out in left center of photo

vulnerable to flood, but rainfall was light. The town only lasted a few years, and the potential danger of flash flood was never tested.

The springs in town furnished water for eight stamp mills and two sawmills. Five smelting furnaces melted down the concentrate produced by the mills. The town boasted a three-story meeting hall, two newspapers, and population of 3,000. Lots sold for as much as $2,000. Rocco Canyon, northwest of town, held a number of paying

A gasoline engine once powered this second-effort crusher mounted below small dam in center of town. Flow of water has dwindled to a trickle, preventing further operation.

Chimney of Shermantown's adobe smelter was apparently never used. Wooden forms still line the flue.

mines. The Great Valley, the Grand Prize, the Homestake, and the Ne Plus Ultra were all sending ore down the road to Shermantown. Ore wagons brought silver chloride down the canyon from Hamilton. Stage coaches hauled the pure silver back up the canyon, through Hamilton and on to Elko for shipment to government mints.

Shermantown's existence was inescapably tied to Hamilton, Treasure City, and Eberhardt. The latter was the site of one of the smallest, richest open-pit silver mines in the world.

When the silver ran out, the mills closed down, and Shemantown lost its reason to exist. By 1880, just eleven years after the town had incorporated, only one family remained.

Today the place is entirely deserted. At the edge of town an adobe chimney stands half completed. Its interior was never blackened by fire. Some forming supports remain inside the combustion chamber. Remains of numerous rock buildings are hidden in the deep sagebrush. Many of the springs have dried up, and their locations can only be determined by the mill wreckage nearby. Much of the water runs underground, providing sustenance to the lush desert growth.

On the flats in the center of the townsite, a small dam has been built to back up water to feed a tiny crusher and shaker. Someone had hopes of separating gold or silver from ore found nearby. Apparently his hopes expired; the machine is rusted and inoperative. The 50,000 miners and prospectors who swarmed over the slopes of the White Pine Mountains apparently found and extracted just about everything of value.

MAP NOTE: The Illipah, Pancake Summit, Green Springs, and Treasure Hill, Nevada, 15 minute United States Geological Survey maps are a proper guide to this area.

PART IV
NEW MEXICO

NEW MEXICO AREA 1

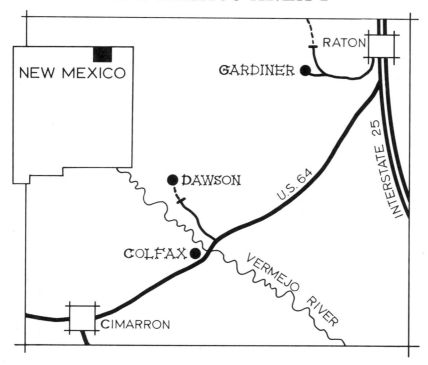

GARDINER, NEW MEXICO

OF THE STRING of perhaps a dozen inactive coal-mining communities in the Raton area, Gardiner is one of the few open to visitation that has enough surviving remnants to make a tour of the grounds worthwhile.

Originally the town was shaped like a capital "L," with one leg extending west along Gardiner Canyon and the other pointing north, parallel to Coal Canyon. The western leg was the residential part of town, while the northern, industrial portion, contained the mines, shops, and coke ovens. The coke ovens, each about twelve feet in diameter, ran in four parallel, red-brick rows, each a quarter of a mile long. More than 300 ovens processed coal from a number of mines that bored into the hill immediately to the west. Tunnel portals dot the hillside, and, from one of the larger openings, heavy cables emerge to lie slack upon the ground. Years ago the cables stretched taunt overhead, supporting buckets that carried waste rock to the dump and coal to the loading chutes. Over the years rainwater has eroded the dumps, adding red streaks of iron oxide to the blues and greens of the waste rock.

Slag heaps and coal piles have washed out to form low mounds on the flats below the mine. The finely powdered coal that usually permeates the building and grounds of active coal towns has been cleansed by rain. Remains of the old lamp house are remarkably clean. The once-blackened stucco appears almost white.

The residential portion of town is sprinkled with foundations, windowless walls, and collapsed roofs. Across the creek a row of adobe walls stands without roofs, apparently the residue of a ravaging fire. Several of the buildings at the center of town seemed to be in livable condition. As I approached, a bearded gentleman emerged from one of the homes and walked toward me.

He was short — just four inches over five feet. He was on the stocky side, carrying a smooth outside curve on the front. His full beard and mustache were silvery white. His nose was small and rounded and his complexion ruddy.

Most of the 300 coke ovens in Gardiner were manned by Italian crews. The Italians were said to be resistant to heat.

Oven was filled with coal and charcoal, then lighted and sealed off with bricks. A day or so later, coke was removed.

He introduced himself as Tom Hay and seemed relieved when I passed up the obvious opportunity to comment on his resemblance to Santa Claus.

Thomas Hay and his 33-year-old son (both bachelors) are the sole residents of town. Being just past sixty years himself, Tom makes no claim of being an old-timer — "at least not for a few years." He has lived in the area since he was eight years old. His folks lived in Brilliant, another ghost town nearby. "We were the last ones to move out of that town, too. Moved from Brilliant down here to Gardiner, now we're the only ones living here.

"Tom pointed down the hill toward some pillars marking the site of a once-imposing structure. "That was the hospital down there. It was pretty fancy compared to most of the buildings. Lot of them were made of adobe." He pointed across the creek. "See those adobe walls? That was the colored section. A big part of the town was Negro. Another part was Italian. They all kept separated." Tom indicated the sections of town. "Over there was a bunch of shotgun

Tom Hay left one ghost town to move to another. Tom and his son are presently the sole residents of Gardiner.

houses — you know — three houses together." Tom swiveled to face his own home. "Live in the old Doc's house now. Not so fancy as the hospital was, but it's still pretty stout."

I opened two well-chilled examples of the brewers' art, fresh from the camper's icebox, and Tom warmed to his subject.

One of the better company houses left on Gardiner's Main Street,
as seen from remains of imposing rock structure.

"The town always was a company town. Used to be an old
S.L.R.M. and P. town. Now Kaiser Steel owns the place.
They own pretty near all the coal towns up and down the
line."

I asked about the abbreviations he had used.

"The St. Louis, Rocky Mountain, and Pacific Company.
They made coke mostly — sold coal too, of course. The coke
was used for smelting copper. That's what killed the town

— someone invented a new way to smelt copper without using coke."

With the evening light gone, I arranged to meet Tom the next day, then headed the three miles back to the town of Raton and the public library, to learn more of the history of Gardiner.

James T. Gardiner was a railroad geologist, ever on the lookout for coal deposits. He inventoried the deposits on the east slope of the hills just west of Raton. The best undeveloped coal deposits were claimed by Gardiner in the name of the Sante Fe Railroad. Others, previously located

Mule drivers lined up for a picture. Coal hauling was considered a step above mining or coking.

Foundations of coal washer fill the foreground.
Lamp house is at the rear.

by Messrs. Pels and Wigham, were obtained by trading land for claiming rights.

In 1881 the Blossburg Mine (later called the Old Gardiner) was in full operation. More mines were opened along the slope, and a number of towns grew around the best producers. Gardiner grew around the coal mine of the same name. Blossburg sprouted two miles to the north. Northwest of Blossburg, up Dillon Canyon, were the towns of Willow and Swastika. The last two towns were later renamed Brilliant I and Brilliant II.

The swastika symbol, made infamous by the Nazi movement in Germany, was earlier considered a good luck sign. Swastikas were laid up in raised brick along the cornice of one of the most imposing buildings in nearby Raton. The symbols were a trademark of the Swastika Coal Company. During the second World War, the owners of the buildings were kept busy explaining just why "those Nazi signs" were up there.

Gardiner had its wild times, in spite of the tight company control of the town. In fact, it was company policy to meet threat with counterthreat, especially in the event of a miners' strike. The biggest strike occurred during the boom years of Gardiner when a thousand folk lived in town and 2,500 miners worked in the area. The company met the strike head-on by sending camp manager Wiggins to Birmingham, Alabama, to hire a troop of Negro workers to come in and break the strike by working in place of the strikers.

Competition for jobs added to racial tensions, and fights occurred with regularity in spite of rigid segregation. The Negroes, Irish, Italians, and whites worked and played separately, merging occasionally to attack or repel an opposing group or combine. Joe Dilisio installed a wooden partition in his saloon to separate the customers. Signs indicated that one side was for "Negroes," the other side for "Cosmopolitans."

No one walked the streets alone after dark. Customers came and went in groups. In spite of such precautions, the number of tombstones and unmarked mounds in the cemetery increased alarmingly.

After World War II, demand for coal decreased rapidly. Coke, once in great demand by copper smelters, was now used in reduced quantities only by a few zinc refiners.

According to Tom Hay, the town of Gardiner had been a near ghost for a number of years before folding completely in 1954. Many of the houses in Gardiner had already been moved to nearby towns. A number of deserted buildings burned down.

When the company packed up all its machinery, right down to the hand tools in the machine shop, the few remaining residents realized that Gardiner was done for.

Now, just twenty years later, coal is on the comeback. Kaiser Steel recently purchased the town. Maybe there is hope for Gardiner yet.

MAP NOTE: Gardiner is shown on the Raton, New Mexico, 15 minute United States Geological Survey topographic map.

DAWSON, NEW MEXICO

When J. B. Dawson bought the land surrounding the
Vermejo River at the point where it leaves the hills and
meanders out upon the flats, he fully expected to receive
1,000 acres for the $3,700 he invested. He bought the land
in 1869 from Lucian Maxwell. The land was part of the old
Beaubien and Miranda Grant Lands now referred to as the
Maxwell Grant.

Dawson's deal with Maxwell was oral — that's the way
Maxwell did business. Dawson had no record of the sale,
and, when called upon to prove ownership, found himself in
danger of losing his thousand acres. Luckily Dawson's
lawyer proved his client's ownership and found records of

Only a few of Dawson's hundreds of homes are left standing.

the transaction in some of Maxell's papers. The land described was not 1,000 acres but 20,000!

Dawson had a particular affection for his holdings. The land had plenty of water, was well-grown with trees and grass, and had an outcrop of high-grade coal. Dawson hated to cut wood and took particular delight in heating his ranch home without laboring on the blister end of an axe handle. Neighbors were soon asking for coal, and before long Dawson's coal sales became more important than raising livestock.

Just after the turn of the century, Dawson and an adjoining neighbor made a deal with a railroad-backed fuel company. In exchange for nearly half a million dollars, the fuel company obtained rights to all the coal and ownership of a section of land for a townsite — later to be called Dawson, of course. Dawson's wife was given exclusive rights to all milk sales in the town for the following ten years.

The mining of coal on a large scale began in 1901. Dawson

Mule barn was made of an early form of cinder block. Mules were brought out of the mines once a month.

numbered 200 citizens by year's end and grew to 600 the following year. By 1903 the town had its own doctor, newspaper, hotel, and fancy theater. By 1905 the population passed the 2,000 mark. When the Phelps Dodge Company took over they expanded operations, and the population jumped to nearly 4,000. Dawson became the largest coal town in the state.

In 1903 a small hint of future disaster was felt when a fire trapped three men in shaft number one. Rescue teams had almost reached the men when explosions rocked the mine. Cave-ins buried the trapped miners. The would-be rescuers, badly burned, escaped with their lives.

Dawson was a model company town, and the mining practices were said to be the most up-to-date in the nation. Since the disaster of 1903, safety had been the motto. Rescue teams won top honors in area competition.

Then, in 1913, disaster struck! Mine No. 2 exploded. Three hundred men were trapped. Rescue teams went into action. Two members died attempting to reach the trapped men. The following day the rescue team brought sixteen men out alive. Shifts of miners, wearing primitive oxygen masks, ventured 3,000 feet down the shaft to help clear the debris leading to the trapped men. Hope soared when a mule was found alive. Efforts were redoubled, and a lone miner was found safe in a side tunnel. But the effort, however heroic, was too late. The missing 263 men were found dead. A special section in the cemetery soon held 263 crosses.

The explosion had been caused by setting off a dynamite blast before the coal dust from the last charge had settled. The coal dust ignited and in turn loosened more dust to form a traveling, roaring inferno that snaked through the shaft, causing cave-ins and releasing pockets of poisonous gas. The traveling detonation ended only when the fires roared out of the tunnel mouth.

Ten years later some mine cars jumped track and knocked down some high-voltage wires. The sudden flash of the electrical discharge was all it took to set off a second traveling explosion of coal dust. One hundred and twenty-two men died, and the crosses in the cemetery, row on row, now numbered a heartbreaking 385.

Fifty years have passed, but standing amid the crosses one can still feel a residue of the sorrow experienced on the two occasions when the whole town stood at graveside.

Pat Garcia felt a different kind of sorrow. Pat and I had

Powerhouse, chimneys, and coke ovens cover a large area at the east edge of Dawson.

taken parallel but separate paths through town. Where I stopped and to take photographs, he stopped and looked, and often dropped his head in thought. I saw him again at a distance, poking about the old coke ovens. At the cemetery we found ourselves leaning on the same fence. He had a poignant story to tell.

Italian headstone demonstrates the cosmopolitan nature of the early citizenry in Dawson. Crosses in background are a small portion of the 385 graves of mine diaster victims.

Pat Garcia was born in Dawson in 1933. He grew up with other miners' kids. He recalled bragging that his dad worked in the "long shaft" — the one that went five miles under the mountain. His childhood was a particularly happy one, especially the years spent in high school. In 1950 Pat left town. That same year, Phelps Dodge, owners of the town and mine, ceased operations. Much of the town was demolished to save taxes.

Now Pat Garcia had returned to the hometown of his childhood. He found his parent's house gone. Indeed, his whole town was gone. Not a single old school pal stood on the corner ready to swap memories. It was as though time had jumped track. For Pat, seventeen years of memories were out of reach, never to be revisited.

MAP NOTE: Dawson is shown on the Cimarron, New Mexico, 15 minute United States Geological Survey topographic map. The 15-minute Koehler, New Mexico, map is necessary to make out the route to Dawson.

COLFAX, NEW MEXICO

Developers of the St. Louis, Rocky Mountain and Pacific Railroad created the town by laying out 2,000 lots. Each lot was 25 feet by 140 feet and priced at $140 each, with discounts for quantity purchases. Lots sold slowly, and the "town" called Vermejo Junction looked like a loser.

In 1908 the New Mexico Sales Company took over and announced that a second railroad would pass through town. In addition, a tract of 40,000 acres of irrigated land was to be made available on the flats below town. The land was touted as ideal for growing sugar beets. At the same

Dickman Hotel at Colfax operated under several names and served a number of purposes. At one time it was a general merchandise store on the first level, with rooms for rent above.

Much planning went into the Colfax Grade School.
Building also served as church.

time, A. C. Cox announced plans to build a multistoried hotel. In spite of the grand plans, lots in town sold slowly. Many agents, when they did sell a few lots, kept the money and skipped town. The January 8, 1909 issue of the *Raton Range* reported that one J. W. O'Brien had sold his holdings in town to other parties and now couldn't be found. Furthermore, it was determined that he had never owned a single one of the lots he sold.

In spite of the small number of residents, Charles Glasgow built a hotel, the Cimarron Lumber Company opened a yard, and a school was built on the hill west of town. A post office was established, and promoters claimed the town was booming. Actually, the town was in a constant struggle to maintain its existence.

Adobe ruins are found just north of the Colfax School.
Rock water tank is in the background.

The post office was shut down in 1921, but the school and the store continued operating. A new sidewalk was laid down in front of the brick store in 1925. In 1927, there was a bit of excitement when a "marauder" reportedly entered town and cut the hose on the lone gas pump.

The school shut down in 1939, and the kids were hauled to classes in Dawson, four miles away. In spite of the closures, promoters claimed the town was growing.

In 1967, when the town was known to be deserted, reporters in state newspapers still claimed 100 citizens. Historian F. Stanley claimed the same year that Colfax was going to be "reborn into activity." He cited the purchase of Dawson by the Kaiser Company. He envisioned many employees of the Kaiser Company building homes in Colfax.

In 1974 the place was completely deserted. However, if you look hard enough you will probably find a report in some newspaper that lots are selling like hot cakes and the population of the town will soon pass the one hundred mark.

MAP NOTE: Colfax is shown on the 1915 Koehler, New Mexico, 15 minute United States Geological Survey topographic map.

NEW MEXICO AREA 2

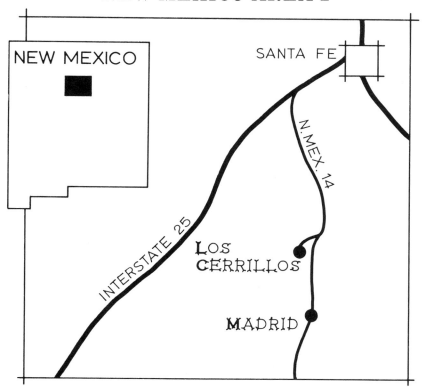

CERRILLOS, NEW MEXICO

MORE THAN TWO THOUSAND YEARS AGO, Indians found deposits of pale blue rock in the little pointed hills by Mount Chalchichuitl. The turquoise was highly valued as a sacred stone capable of protecting its bearer from all evil.

The open pit dug by the Indians in pursuit of the blue charm stone is likely the first mining effort of western man. Measuring 250 feet wide and up to 100 feet deep, the pit was the result of many years of primitive excavation. Stone hammers and wooden wedges were used to loosen projecting rock. Stubborn areas were heated by fire, then fractured with cold water.

The famous Mina del Tiro (Mine of the Shaft) was somewhere in the area, near the open pit. Spaniards using Indian slave labor pursued silver deposits by means of vertical shafts reached by notched log ladders. The digging was confined to horizontal tunnels when the underground water level was reached. Some evidence indicates that skin canoes were used to transport ore at the lowest level. When the Indians rebelled against the Spanish in 1680, the oppressors were killed and the shaft of the Mina del Tiro was filled in. The exact location of the mine has since remained a mystery.

During the 1870s Americans discovered silver in the little hills, and a small boom ensued. It grew to full proportion when the Santa Fe built its tracks through the area in

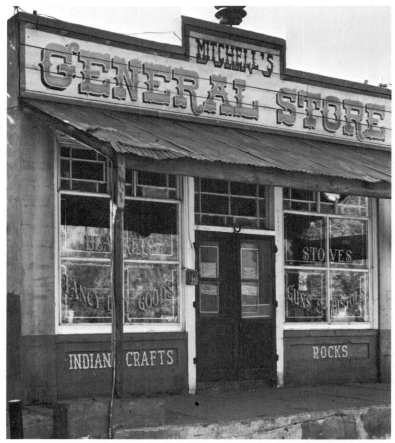

The only store in Cerrillos retains the fancy lettering placed there by a movie company. Owner has changed name at top with a minimum of effort.

1879. Prospectors flooded the region. A camp called Cerrillos grew at the point where the tracks met the Galisteo River. Turquoise was rediscovered, and mining of the semiprecious stone became big business. Nearly a million dollars worth was shipped to market each year during the eighties.

Cerrillos, or Los Cerrillos, grew rapidly during that period. At its peak the town had four hotels, separated by twenty saloons fronting three sides of the town plaza. Tiffany's Saloon became famous for its fine food. The mine of the same name, known for its high-quality turquoise, provided stones for the crown jewels of Spain.

By 1890 Cerrillos had begun its decline. Mining of silver and other precious metals was diminishing, and by 1900 nearly all the mines had folded. The mining of turquoise continued until the 1920s.

Except for the frequent alteration of the outskirts of town by the flooding Galisteo River, Cerrillos has changed little since the mining ceased. The generally dry bed of the Galisteo River comes to life each spring, sometimes overflowing as if in compensation for its brief yearly taste of life. Each year the flood is anticipated, suffered through, then cleaned up after. The center of town stands on high ground and has escaped flood damage. Fire has destroyed some of the places of business, but the remaining buildings fill two sides of the central plaza. Some of the buildings have signs over their doors that seem oddly new and out of place, the result of a brief interruption in the town's quiet history.

Disney Studios chose Cerrillos for the filming of *The Nine Lives of Elfego Baca*. Elfego, a famous New Mexican gunfighter, lived through a barrage of more than 4,000 shots fired over a period of 33 hours, while lying on the floor of a small shack. The gunfight which formed the central theme of the movie actually took place at Frisco, New Mexico. The Disney crew determined that Cerrillos looked more like the "real thing," and proceeded to "improve" it by dressing up the false fronts and tacking up newly painted signs. The owner of the general store has since torn down the board that named the store and reinstalled one that says "Mitchell's," while preserving the large portion that reads "General Store." A sign over one of the hotels still reads "Frisco."

The town comes to life each weekend when visitors from the Santa Fe and Albuquerque areas stop in for a little sightseeing, a meal at Tiffany's, and perhaps an evening at the local opera house.

Luckily I visited town in midweek, when its true nature was displayed. The tourist businesses were closed. The general store was closed, but a sign stated it would open at 10 a.m. Two young boys stood in front waiting for the doors to be unlocked — the only excitement expected in town that morning.

I peeked in the window of the corner saloon. An old man, hand shaded over his eyes, peeked back at me. It was obvious that he lived there and I had infringed on his privacy.

Down the street half a block, a handsome woman stepped

Two elderly residents of Cerrillos died when the rock hotel burned.
Remaining residents then purchased a fire engine.

An abandoned store was renovated to house newly purchased fire engine in Cerrillos.

from the hotel, broom in hand. She smiled, shifted her chew to the other cheek, spat, and said hello.

The storekeeper opened his doors, and a crowd of five or six appeared. The flurry of activity soon ended. Outside, the two young lads wandered over, kicking plumes of dust.

I asked them about the old burned-out rock and dobe building down the block. Yancy Perea answered that it had burned down. "The fire trucks came all the way from Santa Fe — too late — we bought our own fire truck just this year."

Yancy's accent indicated he would be far more at home speaking Spanish. I asked about his pal. "Oh, him? He's Gene — Gene Vick. He's twelve and I'm twelve."

The two youngsters had comments on almost every subject. I learned the details of the last flood (one of the worst ever) and of the new smelter on the hill and that the Tiffany Saloon was 101 years old. Gene proudly read aloud the information sign erected in the plaza. Yancy jumped in where he could.

I commented on the number of long-haired people in town. "Yeah — them hippies. There's almost as many of them in town as there is people!" claimed Gene.

"What do they do for a living?"

Yancy looked up and squinted a bit as if he were giving the question some hard thought. "Some don't do nuthin'." He thought a bit. "Some works." He looked at me seriously. "And some steals." Gene bobbed his head in agreement.

MAP NOTE: The Madrid, New Mexico, 15 minute United States Geological Survey topographic map shows Cerrillos and Mount Chalchihuitl 3 miles to the north.

MADRID, NEW MEXICO

Anthracite, the hard form of combustiable carbon, is found in just three places in the United States: a small area in Pennsylvania, an equally small region in Western Colorado, and strung out along several canyons within five miles of Madrid, New Mexico. The deposits at Madrid are unique in that bituminous, the soft variety of coal, is found adjacent to the anthracite. At the No. 1 mine of the Cerrillos coalfield, bituminous was dug from the left side of the shaft, anthracite from the right.

It was soft coal that attracted the Santa Fe Railway to the head of Waldo Gulch, a few miles north of the tiny settlement of Madrid. In 1882 a spur was run up the canyon

Long rows of unpainted homes still line the streets of Madrid.

a few miles from a point just west of Cerrillos. Madrid continued the mining of coal on a "one mule" scale, while huge quantities of bituminous coal were taken from Waldo Canyon. Soon the demand for the cleaner-burning hard coal grew, and in 1889 the Santa Fe extended the spur to Madrid. New tunnels were dug to reveal seams of both hard and soft coal. Most of Waldo moved to Madrid.

Seven years later the railroad leased its coal-mining operation to the Colorado Fuel and Iron Company of Pueblo, Colorado. The coal seams were difficult to work. Only two to four feet thick, they sloped downward at twenty degrees, at the same time leaning to the side. Mining methods of the time required removal of huge amounts of waste rock. When the main bituminous mine caught fire,

Hotel on the main highway through town once offered board and bed to bachelor miners.

Old 769 was kept busy making the five-mile run to Waldo.
Train hauled coal out and water back to Madrid.

the company gave up what had become a marginal operation. The mines closed without warning, and three
thousand citizens were suddenly without sustenance.

Within a short time George Kaserman, of the Hahn Coal
Company in Albuquerque, bought the operation "town and
all." Under Kaserman's direction Madrid grew to become a
respected company town. New mining methods were employed, and coal production increased steadily over the
years. In 1928 more than 183,000 tons were shipped.

From all indications, Madrid was a great place to live.
Everything in town was owned by the company. All the
houses, the stores, and even the churches were company-
owned. You bought only what the company sold in its
stores, or you went out of town to make your purchase. You

repaired in a company garage the car that you bought from the company store, and you ran it on gasoline the company sold you at prices set by the company. For the most part the prices were fair and the services reasonable.

According to Joe Huber, son of the company superintendent, employees were occasionally "encouraged to go in debt" by purchasing a car or some other expensive item. The management felt that the man would work harder, thus raising coal production. It is also true that it made

Miners' Amusement Hall contained game rooms, clubrooms, and ballrooms. Dues were seventy-five cents per month.

*Catholic Church of Madrid had unusual entrance, with storage
beneath. Structure was stucco-covered adobe and rock.*

switching jobs difficult. You had to pay up before you could
leave. Whatever the viewpoint, the results were the same.

The company did provide a number of valued services for
reasonable fees. Medical expenses cost a mere three dollars a month. The whole family was covered for all medical
needs — except those resulting from fights or childbirth.
Dues in the local club, with access to meeting rooms,
games, entertainment, occasional dances, and frequent
baseball games were just seventy-five cents a month. And
to crown it all, the ultimate in fringe benefits was given

when the company furnished the facilities for employees to brew their own illegal booze during prohibition years!

The increasing availability of natural gas for home heating, and the switch from coal to diesel-fired locomotives, diminished the demand for coal. Mining activities in Madrid decreased with the demand. Madrid's Christmas lights, the finest in the state, were lit for the last time in 1941. In 1954 coal operations, already drastically curtailed, were shut down completely. A few years later only four families lived in a town that once held 4,000.

The number of deserted buildings in town is overwhelming. Most of the buildings are of frame construction. In light of the dry climate, it is surprising that fires have not destroyed most of the town. Part of the business district is fenced off to prevent access, but the fences run only a short distance. Anyone willing to walk a mile or so can freely visit the sites of the old Catholic Church, the large clubhouse, and the many deserted houses that lie on both sides of the dry wash running north through town. A tavern and an outdoor museum are open for business. Both are recommended.

MAP NOTE: The Madrid, New Mexico, 15 minute United States Geological Survey topographic map shows the area in reasonable detail. The site of the old town of Dolores, eight air miles to the southeast, is listed as the Dolores Ranch.

NEW MEXICO AREA 3

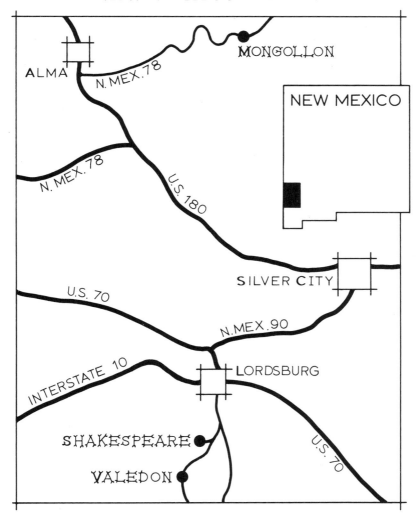

MONGOLLON, NEW MEXICO

THE SIGN STATED that Mongollon was twelve miles and that the road was dangerous for trailers over twenty feet. The first four miles were relatively straight and of gentle slope. Ahead of me, an elderly gentleman towing a trailer experienced no difficulty. Soon the road topped a small rise and entered the left shoulder of a sizable valley. The old gentleman towing the trailer proceeded with only a slight reduction in speed.

Half a mile ahead I could see a smaller trailer coming down the switchbacks. At the first opportunity I passed the trailer ahead of me, and I shortly met the smaller trailer coming down the hill. There was little room to spare. The shoulders of the blacktop were undercut and crumbled. I wondered how the two trailers would fare.

Through the rearview mirror I caught a glimpse of the two rigs stopped in the middle of the road, head-to-head, like two rutting elk prepared to lock horns. Later I learned that both drivers were notably untalented at backing their rigs. Fearing the steep drop-off into the canyon below, they waited — blocking the road for several hours until a driver happened by who could back one of the rigs to a wide spot.

The road is truly spectacular as it hangs on the south

Combination store and smithy at east end of Mongollon
sports a classy false front above patchwork siding.

side of Houston Canyon, then crosses and carves its precarious way along the opposite wall. Soon it gentles and winds north to the slopes of Silver Creek Canyon, where deserted mine structures begin to appear beside the road. Bending around a high knob, the massive tailings and numerous structures of the Fanney Mine (Fannie and also Fanny, take your choice) come into view. The mine is the same height as the road at this point but a mile away and across a canyon more than 600 feet deep.

The road descends sharply, past the ruins of the Last Chance Mine. It crosses a small tributary, then makes a sharp bend to the right. Immediately you are in Mongollon, looking east, up the canyon and up the narrow confines of Mongollon's main street.

Old saloons, boardinghouses, and stores have been renovated to serve as theater, summer residence, and museum.

Both sides of the street are lined with buildings. Under the boardwalks of the buildings on the right, flow the normally gentle waters of Silver Creek. Main Street displays an increasing number of gaps as you travel its quarter mile length. Soon the gaps outnumber the buildings, and the road swings left and begins to climb. Several side streets hacked out of the steep northern slope of the canyon extend parallel to the main street. The road branches at the powder house of the old Fanney Mine. The right branch leads to the cemetery, located on one of the rare deposits of

Fanney Mine was the largest producer in the Mongollon area. Tailings of the mine once slid down canyon, wiping out the Maud S. Mill and damming the creek passing through town.

diggable soil found in an area composed primarily of hard rock. The left branch leads to a long string of deserted houses that ends at the powerhouse and main office of the Fanney Mine.

For a nominal fee you can take a guided tour of the huge complex. A number of unusual sights makes the tour worthwhile: the gigantic opening called "The Big Hole Mike" shaft, the head frame over the 1,400-foot-deep Fanney shaft, the long sorting room with its endless belt, and the lately reworked machine shop used in the recent filming of the movie *My Name is Nobody*. The mine is almost directly above town. Standing on the brink, one must look between his feet to spot the roofs of Mongollon. The prospectors who found the Fanney silver lode must have stood on this spot and enjoyed a similar view.

Sergeant Cooney, leader of a mapping party out of Fort Bayard in 1870, was the first to spot the highly mineralized ledges on Mineral Creek, two miles north of present Mongollon. Cooney was able to suppress his natural Irish tendency to tell the world of his fortunate discovery for almost six years. He kept the secret until he was mustered out. Then, with a few trusted friends, he returned to the discovery. The site was in the middle of hostile Indian territory. The men had barely laid out their claims when the Apaches chased them off their long-held hunting grounds.

Two years later the group returned, greatly reinforced in numbers, weapons, and supplies. Shafts were sunk, cabins built, and Indians repeatedly repelled. In one fracas, Forribeo, son-in-law of Chief Victorio, was shot dead. The chief led a determined counterattack. The miners repelled the onslaught. When fighting slacked, Cooney and a fellow miner headed out to warn people in the nearby town of Alma. The Indians caught up with Cooney and his friends and killed them. The citizens of Alma have since referred to the incident as a massacre. Cooney was buried at the spot, and a memorial was later erected.

Cooney's brother, Captain Michael Cooney, immediately left New Orleans and headed for the newly inherited mine. With his help, the number of mines along Mineral Creek grew, and the small town of Cooney was born. Indian troubles continued, but the weight of numbers was now on the side of the miners. The diggings on Mineral Creek failed to richen with depth, and when a gent named Eberle found some high-grade on Silver Creek in 1889, Cooney Town

The Fanney Mine has changed little since it closed more than thirty years ago.

decamped and the town of Mongollon mushroomed around Eberle's cabin.

Mongollon grew up wild. For fifteen years the law in town was either ineffective or crooked. At one point federal agents were called in to arrest a deputy sheriff. The deputy met the officers with a gun pointed belt high. The feds were fast, however, and in an instant the deputy was stretched out, his blood pooling on the wooden saloon floor. The federal agents left town before a threatened reprisal could be mounted against them.

When outlaws held up the mine payroll and killed two men in the process, citizens quickly formed a posse and galloped in pursuit. One outlaw was killed. The other was captured and returned to town for a short respite before his fate was settled.

Law and order arrived in Mongolon (that's pronounced "muggy-own") in 1914 when town fathers decided to incorporate. The town was then touted as being "the most peaceful in the United States." That's the year the big slide brought the massive tailings of the Fanney down on the buildings of the Maude S. The mill of the Maud S. was reduced to splinters and its watchman buried under tons of yellow silt. The slide continued to the canyon floor, damming the creek and threatening to flood the town. Miners turned out to dig a channel through the slide.

Heavy rain began to fall, and the water rose at an increasing rate. The miners dug faster. When the two efforts

Miners of Mongollon showed great originality. Headboards and crosses in the cemetery were made of slate, concrete – even pipe and electrical conduit.

matched in level, the water poured through the notch, undercut the sides, and quickly washed a channel through the slide.

In spite of the big slide, 1914 was a year of record production. The payroll reached the million-a-year mark, and the town reached its peak population — reported variously to be 2,000, 2,600, and "damn near five thousand." The business district stretched up the canyon for half a mile. Side streets on both sides of the canyon held homes, their second stories level with basements of houses on the tier above.

During the first thirty-seven years of the town's existence, more than eighteen million ounces of silver were mined, refined, poured in ingots, and hauled down the mountain.

In 1931 most observers thought the silver was gone and the town done in, but new discoveries that year brought a flurry of activity. The finds were rich but disappointingly shallow. Mongollon faded again. All mining was suspended when World War II broke out, and Mongollon expired for good.

MAP NOTE: Mongollon and the sites of Cooney, Graham, and Glenwood, are shown on the Mongollon, New Mexico, 1910, 30 minute (½ inch to the mile) United States Geological Survey map.

*Although deeply carved, inscription on old wooden cross
is difficult to make out. The date is 1896.*

SHAKESPEARE, NEW MEXICO

Unbelievable! Born a fake and brought to a boom by a fraud, Shakespeare was raised to a second frenzied peak by con artists who made utter fools of the original perpetrators. Throw in a number of hangings, a few bizzarre incidents, and cap it with a grand old lady standing off condemnation by the state of New Mexico, and you have a story seldom equalled in fiction.

Back in 1867 the place was called Mexican Springs. "Uncle" Johnny Evensen built a crude structure by the water hole and called it a stage station. It was used occasionally when the stage had to pass up its regular stops due to Indian trouble.

When a second citizen moved in with Evensen, the two of them decided the place needed a more dignified name, like Grant.

Occasional prospectors passed through. Some even checked the hills for mineral deposits. One of them. W. D. Brown, filed a claim and took some "typical" samples to San Francisco for "promotional purposes." He showed the samples to William C. Ralston, head mogul of the Bank of California. Ralston had the samples assayed. The report came back (it was reported) at 12,000 ounces of silver per ton!

Quickly Ralston staked claims adjacent to the find. He then extended the streets of Grant, laid out lots, and named the whole shebang Ralston City. It was easy for banker Ralston to start the rush to Ralston. He simply capitalized a company and sold stock while spreading rumors of even greater assay reports.

When the shallow deposits of silver began to fade, Ralston quietly left town, his fortune doubled. The losers drifted off, and Ralston became a ghost town, population of two — old Uncle Johnny Evensen and his pal. The two leading citizens of town were about to change the name back to Grant when a couple of prospectors showed up, all shifty-eyed and secretive. They wanted to put some bags of valuables in Evensen's vault. Somehow they let it "slip" that the bags were full of precious gems. With a little prodding from Uncle Johnny, the two prospectors opened up. They had discovered a diamond field, by God! They were on their way to San Francisco to get some financial backing. They had a gent named Ralston in mind.

Ralston was interested but suspicious. He had the stones appraised at Tiffany's, then hired a mining expert he could trust. Tiffany's reported the diamonds were the real thing, and the mining expert returned from a guided tour of the area in an ecstatic condition. He had found diamonds on ant hills, in pack rat holes, and even on top of the ground!

Ralston paid the mining expert a handsome fee and promptly bought the diamond field for $600,000. Out to redouble his fortune, he again capitalized a company and proceeded to sell shares. When false rumors got out that the diamonds were in southwestern New Mexico, prospectors and promoters deduced the location and promptly started a second rush to Ralston City. Within weeks of the first diamond stock sales, hundreds of newcomers had descended on Uncle Johnny's stage station. Within a month new saloons were thrown up and another hotel hastily built. Three thousand people wintered in Ralston, drinking it up on cold days, otherwise searching the hills in vain for the fabulously rich diamond field.

Some folk who had been taken on Ralston's earlier schemes chose to investigate his latest stock promotion. It wasn't long before Clarence King, government inspector and geologist, showed up in Ralston's office. King and his assistant were given secret directions to the site. It turned out to be in Summit County, Colorado, nowhere near booming Ralston City.

The inspector found a few diamonds — all of them suspiciously on the surface. Digging in the area produced only dirt. King's assistant made one spectacular find — a diamond with some polished facets. King sent word to Ralston that the field was a fake. The huckster had been had. His stock collapsed, and he was put under investigation for fraud. Ralston eventually went broke and reportedly committed suicide.

The town of Ralston continued to boom for a while. Residents refused to believe it had all been a hoax. After all, Ralston's offices were a thousand miles away, and the so-called salted field was way up in Colorado. Prospectors continued to search for the diamonds in the hills near Ralston City.

Eventually the promoters left town, followed later by the prospectors. The hard cases remained, rustling cattle here and there for subsistence. Ralston City became an outlaw town.

A few of the mines near town still held paying ore, but

Ralston City's fraud-filled reputation precluded any chance of financing. Two Englishmen, Colonel William Boyle and his brother, General John Boyle, were well aware of the silver ore left in the Bonnie Jean and Jenny Boyle mines. They waited a few years to let memories dim, then quietly snapped up the two mines and the town of Ralston.

They renamed the town Shakespeare, a proper English name, gathered a small quantity of choice ore, and headed west for financing. There were modestly successful, and Shakespeare grew slowly. In 1879 the town had a post office (Uncle Johnny was postmaster), a couple of saloons, a growing number of solid citizens, and the Stratford Hotel. The solid citizens occasionally became disenchanted with some of the outlaw types still hanging around, and drastic action was sometimes required.

Arkansas Black was a popular fellow. He operated the Silver Dollar Saloon, and everything would have been all right if his operations had stopped there. It was his extracurricular activities with the married women in town that angered the men, and it was the last straw when Arkansas was found in bed with the wife of one of Shakespeare's better-known citizens. Arkansas was confronted and told to leave town. He resisted but was overpowered. Shakespeare's first vigilante committee had trouble convincing him that he had to leave. He had always been a popular guy and wasn't inclined to take the threats seriously. The menfolk eventually resorted to a little neck-stretching to get his undivided attention. After each short suspension, they lowered Arkansas and asked him if he would agree to leave town. Each time, between gasping breaths, he croaked a refusal, mixed with an assortment of selected cusswords. The last time they strung him up, Arkansas went limp. Quickly he was lowered. A bucket of water was thrown in his face. Arkansas came to, fighting mad! He demanded a six shooter, asking the chance to fight it out like a man.

The vigilantes admired the man for his guts, and besides, not a one of them cared to volunteer to oppose him in a fair fight. After a little serious discussion, the committee decided he wasn't such a bad guy after all. The fault lay with the wicked woman who had enticed him. The woman was given notice, and the problem was solved.

Very likely, Arkansas Black was a member of the vigilante party that took Russian Bill and Sandy King from the local jail in order to expedite justice. There was no talk this time — just straight ropework. In minutes the two outlaws hung from the crossbeam in the main room of the Grant House. Breakfast at the hotel was delayed next morning while the bodies were cut down and hauled out for burial.

Later Johnny Evensen answered an inquiring relative's inquiry by stating that Russian Bill had died of throat trouble. Johnny graciously failed to mention anything about horse stealing or midnight ropework.

The silver panic of 1893 brought mining to a halt in Shakespeare. By this time a small community called Lordsburg had grown up just three miles away on the Southern Pacific tracks. Most of Shakespeare moved to the new town. A few folk moved a mile in the other direction to a community growing around new activity at the "85" Mine, an early mine that had been revitalized by the generous use of dynamite to expose new ore.

In 1914 a spur was run from Lordsburg to the "85," and the tracks were put right through the town of Shakespeare — right down the center of deserted main street — an unwarranted insult to a dying town.

But that wasn't quite the end of Shakespeare's impossible story. In 1935 Frank and Rita Hill bought the town. They reconditioned one of the better buildings as a ranch house and proceeded to run stock on the acreage bought along with the town.

The Hills restored the old town and opened it to tourists. Rita Hill wrote up the history of the town in a fascinating booklet entitled *"Then and Now, Here and There Around Shakespeare."* Later, when daughter Janaloo grew up, she and her father rode horseback to San Diego and back, publicizing the old ghost town. Rita and Janaloo continued to run the spread alone after Frank passed away.

Recently the New Mexico Highway Department condemned a strip of land extending through the Hills' acreage. The new superhighway would effectively separate their cattle from the water supply.

The condemned strip would just about ruin the ranch. Rita decided to ask the highway department to at least dig a well on the isolated land and provide an underpass for access.

The highway department refused. Rita and Janaloo decided to do battle. They refused to accept the $33,221.59 for the condemned fifty-nine acres. They picketed the state legislature. They refused to sign any agreement with the highway department. All was to no avail. In late November of 1973, the judge ruled against Rita Hill, found her in contempt, and fined her $3,000. She was given notice to vacate the land in three months.

Rita and Janaloo weren't quitting yet. They moved a tiny seven-by-eight-foot stucco shack onto the highway land and planted it smack in the middle of the spot where

Access to the old town of Shakespeare has been limited since owner, Rita Hill, lost her crusade against the New Mexico Highway Department.

Ramp C was to join Interstate 10. Rita lived in the shack for three months — right up to the deadline of November 23.

Newsmen and onlookers watched as sheriff's deputies cajoled, coaxed, then threatened. Eventually the door of the shack was shoved in, and 71-year-old Rita Hill was read her rights and arrested. Rita was placed in jail and told she would remain there until she signed the release papers. On December 10, Rita signed the paper and was released. She still refused payment for the land. She did authorize lawyers' fees to be taken from the fund, but $19,000 still remains on deposit unclaimed by Rita Hill.

Disenchanted with the effects of progress and frustrated by the impersonal nature of legal condemnation, Rita and her daughter have retreated to their home in Shakespeare.

Recently Rita Hill locked the gate to the town of Shakespeare; it is no longer open to visitors. There was no other way she could register her resentment. I cannot help but agree with Rita Hill. This book shows only one photograph of the town of Shakespeare. Somehow it wouldn't seem right to show more.

MAP NOTE: The Lordsburg, New Mexico, 7½ minute and 15 minute maps cover the area.

VALEDON, NEW MEXICO

The 1932 Lordsburg topographic map showed a dozen buildings at Shakespeare. About a mile to the south the map indicated nearly 200 buildings under the name of

Henry Clay Mine stands idle in front of remains of Valedon. Old "85" Mine, just above schoolhouse at left, is still operating.

Several company stores occupied this long, rock building in Valedon's business district.

Valedon. A tramway was shown connecting the railroad to a point a mile and a half west.

The 1963 map of the same area showed only five empty structures in Shakespeare. The tramway was missing on the map, and, oddly, Valedon was shown with just two buildings. The cartographer was either in great error on on one of the maps, or something drastic had happened to Valedon.

I inquired about Valedon at a small highway cafe in Lordsburg. The waitress, the manager, and several on-lookers all assured me, with some heat, that there never was a town of Valedon. When shown the maps, they were sure the maps were wrong and began to suspect I was attempting some sort of hoax.

The local newspaper office furnished some information on the town of Shakespeare. When asked about Valedon, the editor answered she had heard of it but had never been there.

With great expectations I drove the short mile from

Most of the buildings in Valedon were blown up to save taxes. Walls of store and superintendent's home (above) survived the blast.

Shakespeare to Valedon. As I broke over a small rise I was confronted with a barren bowl surrounded by jagged hills. I could see a few old mine structures and one small mine still operating.

Upon closer inspection I could make out a number of buildings blending in with the background. As I drove closer, the remains of Valedon came clear, and they were considerable.

There were some "no" signs about, so I headed for the operating mine to gain permission to look the old town over. Ramon Renteria was willing to interupt his work for a few minutes. In fact, he was quite tickled to have someone ask about Valedon.

"I was born here. Right here in Valedon, in 1917. Yes, it was a pretty decent town — that was the school over there, theater there, and those long rock buildings — they were stores."

Ramon's boss drove up. There was a slight pause, then the two of them began pointing out the sights of the town. The superintendent's house had been up on the hill; now only foundations are left. The mine down in the bottom was the old Henry Clay. Up on the hill was the old Atwood Mine.

They presently had thirty-five men working two shifts in the "85" Mine. They were tunneled in 800 feet, then down 1,950 feet. Ramon's boss gave the okay for me to look the old buildings over but gave me firm warning to look out for open shafts and rattlesnakes. "Ramon killed five rattlers down in the draw by the store just yesterday."

The "85" Mine now operating was one of the first mines ever to be worked in the area. Sam Ransom, Shakespeare blacksmith, staked out the claim sometime in the 1890s. It wasn't until 1907 that someone shot off a bundle of dynamite in the tunnel and uncovered some decent ore.

The new owners hired a crew and began stockpiling the ore. Soon other claims in the area were found to contain profitable ore, and the number of miners increased. Within a year, the mines around the "85" were employing nearly 100 men.

Most of the miners walked the three and a half miles to and from Lordsburg each day. A few of them took up residence in nearly deserted Shakespeare. Several of Shakespeare's saloons went back into business as halfway houses. They attracted most of the miners going off shift, and probably some of those going on shift. Within a year a tent town grew around the "85," and, before the second winter, a number of boardinghouses were built. Eventually streets were laid out, and the community became the town of Valedon.

When the railroad spur connected the town with the main line at Lordsburg in 1914, Valedon quickly grew to more than 1,000. Valedon was a company town and tightly controlled as to drinking and general hell-raising. Shakespeare, less than a mile down the tracks, was the perfect sin town. That town was at least consistent. Somehow it always played host to the violent, the crooked, or the fraudulent. Its wickedness kept Valedon relatively chaste.

Faro wheels, blackjack, and poker games were all-night attractions in the basements of the saloons in Shakespeare. One evening a general fight broke out. When the survivors took inventory, they found a number of people laid out either by alcohol or violence. One man failed to respond and after close inspection was found to be dead. No one had the slightest idea who was responsible. Lacking a better solution, the body was laid out on the tracks running down main street. The railroad reported the death as an "unfortunate accident."

Two Negroes stopped by Shakespeare on their way to their mine on Lee's Peak, two miles west of Valedon. As they paid for their supper, some of the hard cases in town took note of the wads of money the two men carried. The money was the payroll for the miners working at the shaft owned by the two blacks. The crooks caught up with the men, beat them to death, and searched the bodies for the money. None was found. Apparently the two had stashed the payroll somewhere just outside of town. Since that event, the wash heading to Lee's Peak has been called the Arroyo de los Negros.

Things were not always completely respectable in Valedon. Lyman Garrett, brother of the famous Pat Garrett and sheriff of Valedon, was found one morning lying in front of his jail. Citizens assumed that Garrett had been jailing some law violators when they somehow took his gun and, fearful of the sound of shots, chose to beat the sheriff to death. Two men were apprehended for the crime and subsequently convicted.

The town of Valedon boomed from 1920 to 1927. The population grew to more than 2,000. Permanent stores lined the streets, and a modern school was constructed. During the boom years, a threatened railroad strike was averted when leading supporters of the two factions (labor union

*Huge opening leads to smaller shaft just below
the Atwood Mine at outskirts of Valedon.*

and mine management) agreed to face off in a boxing
match. It was a long, well-balanced fight. Both parties
ended the fight with serious injuries. Apparently it cooled
the strike to the point where mediation seemed preferable.

The Great Depression brought mining to a halt in 1932.
The owners, Phelps Dodge, in accordance with standard
company practice, summarily ordered the citizenry to vacate. The town was then dynamited to save on taxes. The
school building was left intact as a possible future company office. The stoutly built rock and brick buildings lost
their roofs, but the walls were left standing. Dynamite to

finish the job would cost more than the added tax savings that would result from their complete eradication.

It was now clear just why the 1932 map showed a full-blown town (pardon the pun) and the 1963 map showed only two buildings.

MAP NOTE: The Lordsburg, New Mexico, 1932, 15 minute United States Geological Survey topographic map shows the town of Valedon intact. The Lordsburg, New Mexico, 1963, 7½ minute map shows the town after destruction.

PART V
COLORADO

COLORADO AREA 1

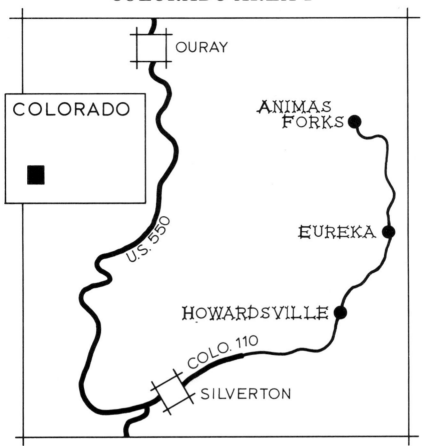

COLORADO

OURAY

ANIMAS FORKS

U.S. 550

EUREKA

HOWARDSVILLE

COLO. 110

SILVERTON

HOWARDSVILLE, COLORADO

THE ROCKY PROMINENCES of a dozen peaks rise to more than 14,000 feet. Cascading streams fill the narrow floors of deep valleys. Trails into the area hang on steep mountainsides and cross unstable talus slopes. The passes giving access are more than two miles above sea level. Some remain snow-covered the year around. Where the snow melts, avalanches are common. It is a difficult land to traverse.

From Silverton the road heads northeast up the valley of the Animas River. As the valley narrows, the road, by necessity, imitates the river's every bend and sweep. In four miles the valley opens, and the road crosses the now gently meandering stream.

A few old cabins lie sprinkled across the valley. The remains of an old mill stand on the flat at the north edge of town. An aerial tramway still extends from the mill, reaching upward in broad dips toward a mine now hidden by tall trees. Rusted ore buckets hang at random intervals. The cable extends through the mill, passes around a weighted turnabout wheel, then returns through the mill and back up the slope. The mill is guyed with an opposing cable to

Weathered old mill is the most impressive remnant in Howardsville.

Anchor cable counteracted toppling effect of aerial tramway.

balance the toppling pull of the tramway. The equalizing effect of the anchor cable is controlled by a series of pulleys mounted in blocks to increase sevenfold the force applied.

Captain Baker, prospector and explorer, led the first party of gold seekers into the area. The seven-man party set out in July of 1860 determined to explore the San Juan (St. John) River. Finding little color in that drainage, the party moved to the northwest. Gold in sand was finally located in modest quantity at the confluence of Cascade Creek and the Animas River. Baker sent out exaggerated reports, and that December, Kellogg, one of the financial backers of the original group, brought in a party of one hundred. Many of the prospectors brought their families. Winter travel in the high mountains was chancy, and the party barely survived a severe blizzard encountered in San Luis Park. Members of the party found it necessary to burn their wagon boxes and furniture in order to keep warm.

By the following May a camp was established at a site referred to as Animas City, but poor-paying sand and threatening Indians caused rampant dissatisfaction and desertion. Everyone blamed Baker for exaggerating the original strike, and at one point they threatened to hang him.

Within a few months Animas City was nearly deserted. A gentleman named Pollack remained until fall, surviving the threats of the Utes by donating (under duress) precious goods to the Indians. In return he was given four Navajo children held captive by the Utes. Eventually war broke out, and the Indians warned all whites to clear out of the surrounding area.

Baker returned with another party in 1868. Again he failed to live up to his claims of riches, and most of his party deserted. Baker and two faithful friends headed southwest, hastened on their way by hostile Indians. Cornered in a canyon, the trio had no choice but to build a raft of driftwood and float down the stream. The stream was the Colorado, and the point of launch was the head of the Grand Canyon. Baker was shot dead as the raft was pushed off. One of the remaining two men was washed overboard and drowned. The last man survived by lashing himself to the raft. He was found days later and miles downstream, still bound to the raft — unconscious, but still alive.

Streets were laid out by the Bullion City Company in 1874 at the junction of Cunningham Creek and the Animas River. The town was named Bullion City by the promoters. New residents changed the name to Howardsville at the first town meeting, probably for a man named Howard who had built the first cabin in town.

Silverton was springing up at the same time, but Howardsville, somewhat larger, was selected as county seat. Within a year, however, Silverton's promoters were claiming a population of 3,000. Recorded figures indicated that 800 was a lot closer to the truth, but, whatever the population, Silverton outshown its neighboring city, and the seat was transferred by majority vote of the citizenry of the two towns.

Niegoldtown and Highland Mary, both smaller than Howardsville, grew up around large mine and mill complexes. Both towns were on Cunningham Creek within five

Main cable of tramway reversed direction by
passing around the turnabout wheel.

miles of Howardsville. They did little to preserve
Howardsville's population. In 1877 Howardsville had four
saloons, a brewery, a reputation, and a population that
showed up mostly on weekends.

In 1881 Howardsville could muster a mere 150 on election day. The town died slowly as mine after mine shut
down. The post office finally closed in 1939. Presently, two
or three cabins are occupied, and one mine sends ore to a
modern mill at the east end of town.

The Highland Mary Mine and town, south of Howardsville, has its own unique history. The two Ennis Brothers
of New York City, recipients of a large inheritance, decided
they would like to invest their money in a gold mine. Dev-
out believers in the occult, they logically consulted their
favorite seer as to where that gold might be found. The
seer, primed with a fat fee, pored over a map of the west.

His hand descended on Colorado. A map of Colorado was quickly obtained. The seer strained to the utmost and, after much concentration, plunked his finger on the map at the spot where great riches would be found. The spot was on a high pass five miles from Howardsville at an elevation of 11,200 feet. The believing brothers staked out the claim

Hoist bar and old cabin are backdropped by Macomber Peak and Dome Mountain. Hematite Lake is just over the notch.

and recorded it as the Highland Mary. For an added fee, the spiritualist wandered over the area and "sensed" the lodes.

Several years and a million dollars later, the disillusioned brothers sold out and returned east. The new owners dug along the thin veins of ore. The veins joined, and rich deposits were located. The mine became a strong producer but a short-lived one. In a few years the town, mine, and mill collapsed. At present the mill foundations are about all one can find at the site. It's a great place to picnic and a rewarding place to snoop about. The hillsides between Highland Mary and Howardsville are crowded with remnants of the mining boom. Numerous cables still scallop their way up the 2,000-foot eastern scarp of the valley. Buildings of the Little Fanney Mine perch midslope with little evidence of support. Nearby, tramway buckets of the Buffalo Boy swing a hundred feet in the air — still loaded with ore.

MAP NOTE: The Silverton, Colorado, 15 minute and the Howardsville, Colorado, 7½ minute United States Geological Survey topographic maps show Howardsville and most of the old mines in the area.

EUREKA, COLORADO

The Sunnyside Mine was Eureka's prime reason for being. The town, like the mine, sputtered reluctantly into existence, ran well for a time, then slowed and clattered to an apparent halt. Then, like an overheated engine, it banged out a few more revolutions, gasped, and died.

Three thousand claims were filed in Animas Valley during 1873. Few of the claims were proved up and, of those, few payed off. The Sunnyside, located three miles northwest and a half mile above Eureka, was a notable exception.

George Howard located the Sunnyside in 1873. The tunnel followed the vein into the mountain just above Lake Emma. The direction of the vein indicated that it would outcrop again on the other side of the hill. Inspection led to the discovery of the Sunnyside extension (later called the

*Miners' shacks at Eureka were placed well out on the flats
to escape snowslides spawned by barren slopes.*

Stout timbers indicated this small structure served originally as a water tower and was later adapted to other use. Sunnyside Mill ruins are in the background.

Gold Prince), just three-quarters of a mile northeast and at the identical elevation of the original strike. The vein held ore of reasonable quality. The melt obtained was seventy percent gold, twenty percent silver, and ten percent lead.

John Terry provided much of the early finances, but his input exceeded the yield and he was forced to sell. He got a good price but was given only $75,000 down, with payments to follow over a number of years. The new owners found the mine to be a loser and refused to make further payments. With the $75,000 and the help of Rasmus Hanson, Terry again took over the mine and turned the Gold Prince into a paying proposition. At one time it was acclaimed the richest mine in the state and was eventually to yield over $50 million in gold and silver.

Meanwhile, back down the hill at the flat spot below the

Unnamed mine hangs precariously at top
of talus slope just east of Eureka.

confluence of Niagara Creek and the Animas River, a town
was taking shape. The town was officially platted in 1874,
or 1887, or 1881, depending on who wrote the town's history. However, it is certain that the town was platted and a
land patent applied for. Some years later, after an un-
explainable delay, the town patent was issued. It was
dated 1883 and signed "Chester A. Arthur, President."

By this time the town had more than four dozen homes
and a business district to match. The *San Juan Expositor*

Large boardinghouse at north end of Eureka is poorly located. Spring floods and winter snowslides threaten building annually.

was publishing the news, but competition from other sheets in the region kept the *Expositor* from turning out more than one issue a month.

Residents took care to build their homes in the center of the broad gravel flat, hoping that rockfalls and snowslides would expend their energies at the fringes. The town was to remain free of damage, but surrounding mines and shacks were frequently covered, moved, or eliminated by avalanches.

The Silver Wing bunkhouse was swept away in 1906. The body of one victim was being moved for burial when a storm hit the area. The body was left by the road while the relatives took cover. Later the corpse was found buried under another avalanche. Apparently the man's number was up.

Deep drifts all but eliminated traffic during the winter. Postmen wearing snowshoes brought in the mail and as much meat as their backs could handle. With freight hauling curtailed due to deep drifts, the price of meat soared, and the moonlighting mailmen seized the opportunity. Eighty pounds was an ordinary load.

On one occasion a postman disappeared with a bundle of mail containing pay vouchers and other valuables. He was never heard from again. When a second postman turned up missing, it was assumed he had also absconded. Two years later the second postman's body was found, quite well preserved, in a snowbank, where he had been swept off the trail and buried by an avalanche.

The broad flats of Eureka show little evidence of the two thousand people who once lived here. A few log shacks, extensive mill foundations, and a nearly intact tramway are the most obvious. In the center of the townsite a small but tall building seems to defy definition. It looks like a hose tower, but it's not tall enough. The stout timbers at the corners and in the center would imply a water tower, but the area under the roof is not large enough. It could have been an overhead loader, but there is no evidence of a ramp. Perhaps it was originally a water tower and was later decapped and used for storage.

Half a mile north of town, in a deep narrow valley, is a large dormitory of relatively recent vintage. Probably it was last used by Sunnyside miners. It is poorly located and could be wiped out any winter by avalanche or any spring by flood, but while it lasts it is spectacular.

Southeast of town, half way up the forty-five-degree

*In spite of its precarious location, old boardinghouse
shows signs of recent renovation.*

slope of Crown Mountain, a ramshackle old mine structure
clings, defying all of Isaac Newton's postulations. The
topographic map of the area fails to show a name for the
mine. The cartographers probably figured the structure
would be gone by the time the maps were published.

The Sunnyside Mine died hard. At one time it was the

largest mine in the state, and ores from its tunnels fed four
different mills, all running continuously. But there never
was a vein that didn't end. The Sunnyside closed down in
1931.

A few folk stayed on in hopes the mine might be
reopened. Their hopes were realized in 1937, when fifty
men were hired to refit the mill. The population climbed
from nearly none to almost a hundred, and Eureka laid
claim to being the second largest town in the county. Hopes

*Old wagon axle lies partly awash. Animas River, gentle in
summer, can rampage during spring runoff.*

faded when work on the reconditioning slowed. The town lost its post office in 1939 and prospects for survival looked bleak again. But in 1940 the machinery at the mill was finally put in motion, running "smooth as glass." Ore stockpiled on dumps was processed, and reserves in the mines were blocked out. However, Law 208 forced the mine out of production in 1942, when all gold mining was declared nonstrategic. Manpower was needed for the war effort. In 1948 the mill was sold for salvage, and the huge complex was quickly dismantled.

The town of Eureka is deserted. The Animas River wanders through town, changing course at will, occasionally undermining and toppling another of the remaining structures. Debris lines the banks. A plank here, a gallows wheel there — and, half buried in the gravel, the front axle of an old freight wagon. Only the bare bones of Eureka remain, and these will not long withstand the double-edged threat of avalanche and flood.

MAP NOTE: The Handies Peak, Colorado, 7½ minute United States Geological Survey topographic map shows Eureka and the various mines mentioned in the text.

ANIMAS FORKS, COLORADO

In spite of the offer of free lots, there was no great rush to build homes in Animas Forks. The 11,200-foot elevation and heavy winter snows made life difficult and the necessities of that life expensive. Summers were pleasant but winters were lonely, and one could be locked in by snow for months at a time. The operators of the San Juan Smelting

Most pretentious house in Animas Forks was the home of Tom Walsh, discoverer of the Camp Bird Lode near Ouray.

Hills around Animas Forks are occasionally snow-covered even in midsummer. View from porch of fancy house overlooks a similar residence, the Animas River, and remains of Columbus Mine and Mill.

Company Mill at the junction of the two forks of the Animas River wanted to maintain continuous operations but were plagued by dwindling work forces each fall. The free lots helped attract a few, but it was the opening of more mines and the building of a number of additional mills that brought Animas Forks into full four-season existence.

That was in 1877, and it wasn't long before the forested hillsides had been cut bare for winter firewood. The mayor of the budding town warned the residents that, without trees, avalanches would be free to roll into town.

He was right, but his forecast was a bit early. Major

Houghton Mountain, source of many snowslides,
overlooks the old mill below Columbus Mine.

avalanches did not occur at the town proper until the turn
of the century. However, the threat of the surrounding
mountains was ever present, and mines located on their
slopes were frequently endangered. Houghton Mountain
to the northwest, California Peak to the southwest, and
Cinnamon Mountain to the east, all more than 13,000 feet
high, collected massive amounts of snow.

At its peak, Animas Forks had two assay offices, one
hotel, a stout jail, and a few fancy houses built by mine
owners. Most of the miners lived in large boardinghouses
at the mine sites another 1,000 feet above town. The town
had enough saloons to occupy miners on weekends.

English sparrows arrived in the valley during the sum-

*The Bagley Mine complex as seen through
the remains of the Columbus Mine.*

mer of 1896. They had been noticed in Denver in 1892. Their
migration rate westward was calculated at fifty miles per
year.

The mines and mills, and hence the town, began to fade
in the early nineties. As was often the case, efforts were
made to get a railroad in to lower the cost of transporta-
tion, thus making possible the processing of lower-grade
ore. As a consequence, Otto Mears extended the railroad
from Eureka. To do so, he had to lay the tracks on the
wagon road in several narrow spots. One four-mile stretch
contained seven areas badly prone to blockage by snowslides. The unsinkable Otto, who had built roads and railroads across terrain others termed impossible, proceeded
to build "avalanche proof" deflectors. Great claims were
made about the strength of the design. The first avalanche
wiped them out. The railroad was completed in 1906, minus
the avalanche guards.

That winter brought some of the worst storms in the
town's history. It snowed steadily for a week. Snowslides
killed twenty people in outlying communities — thirteen

alone in the Shenandoah Boardinghouse that was swept downhill, reduced to rubble, and permanently buried in the debris. One avalanche filled a miner's shack with snow, removed it from its original site, then covered it with fifty feet of the "white death." The miner managed to dig his way out, cutting steps as he followed the fissures in the snow. Many slides rode down the mountains southeast of town, crossed the stream and the road, then climbed the opposite hill. Witnesses claimed the top of the slide would curve back on itself like a tidal wave, then fall back down toward the river.

In 1917 the huge Gold Prince Mill was dismantled and moved to Eureka. By 1926 the town of Animas Forks was deserted.

Now only one mill and a dozen residences are standing at the townsite. In a small building at the base of the remaining mill, hundreds of sacks of cement, all hard as rock,

Several buildings of the Bagley Mine, just west of Animas Forks, were wiped out by recent snowslides.

*Fresh snow adds a dappled beauty to log dam across the Animas River,
a mile or so downstream from the town of Animas Forks.*

stand in evidence of great hopes unfulfilled. Upstream a half mile on the west fork are the extensive buildings of the Bagley Mine complex.

I visited the site in mid-June. It had snowed eight inches the day before, but now it was warm and the snow was melting. Numerous rockslides cracked down the slopes. Rock chucks scrambled about, escaping their water-logged retreats to enjoy the sun. Water ouzels, commonly called dippers, were present in unusual numbers — some walking the river bottoms competely submerged, others standing on rocks convulsively bouncing up and down, busily living up to their nickname.

MAP NOTE: Animas Forks and adjacent towns are shown on the Handies Peak, Colorado, 7½ minute United States Geological Survey topographic map.

Dilapidated main street of Animas Forks shows a
variety of construction and renovation.

COLORADO AREA 2

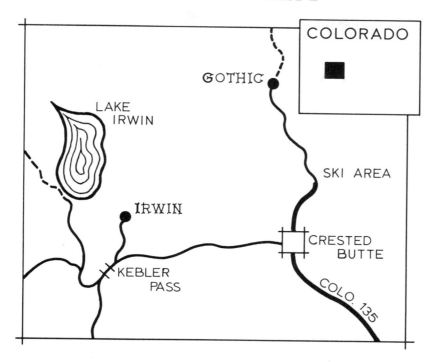

IRWIN, COLORADO

THE MT. AXTELL and the Oh-Be-Joyful topographic maps
need to be joined together to give a complete picture of the
Irwin townsite. A rectangle, three-quarters by three-
eighths of a mile adjacent to Irwin Lake (once called Bren-
nan Lake) is labeled on the maps as Irwin Corporate Body.
Along this stretch of land and extending to the south a bit
into an area once called Ruby, was the mile-long main
street of the short-lived silver boomtown of Irwin.

I could find little sign of buildings as I walked up the
boulder-strewn road. There was nothing left of the seventy
business houses that once lined the main street. Twenty-
three of those business places had been saloons. There
wasn't a sign of their existence — no bottles, no smashed
kegs, not even a lonely rusted barrel hoop.

As I walked the area, faint signs of old foundations became evident, and down by the stream I spotted several
shacks. Across the creek and up the hill were the extensive

Little log cabin of Irwin, Colorado, is dwarfed by tall trees.

The Forest Queen Mine, biggest silver producer in the Ruby Range.

and nearly intact remains of the old Forest Queen Mine, once the biggest producer in the area. The owner of the mine was once offered a million dollars for it — and he refused to sell. In 1932 it sold for $40.45 in back taxes.

The mine showed signs of occupation. An old steam tractor was blocked in position to provide power for some of the mine machinery. It was rusted and in disrepair. Next to the tractor, a vintage car was tilted at an odd angle, its rear end jacked up and pointed toward the shaft house like a skunk ready to do business. A belt led from a rear tire to a pulley wheel on a dewatering pump. Another car was "reared up" and connected by belt to an ore crusher. On the other side of the structure an old army weasel was mounted by the cable-hoisting drum. A number of short iron rods connected the trackless left rear sprocket of the weasel to the flywheel of the defunct steam engine once used to raise the skip. The flywheel was connected to the cable drum.

The door of the adjacent cabin stood open, and a sign on the table read, "Please sign the register. I'm working on a ditch up by the lake." The cabin was neat, and its shelves were lined with canned goods. I signed and went looking for the mechanical wizard who was responsible for all the Rube Goldberg innovations.

I drove down to the junction and took the main road to the lake. There I crossed a ford and headed up a slippery mud road, looking for the ditch and hence the mine owner. My pickup was in four-wheel drive, superlow, when it failed to make the last muddy hill. After a short sideways slide I got the vehicle headed back down. I realized I had

Steam tractor was used to power support machinery at the Forest Queen.

Powered by a converted World War II weasel, cable hoist of Forest Queen is still operable.

made the only recent tracks and that no one was up that hill anyway.

Back at the mine John Hahn and Barry Davis, the two I had sought in vain, were finished with their ditch work and were relaxing over a cup of coffee. I was invited to help empty the pot.

John Hahn, a retired colonel, served in the artillery for thirty years. He had always had a desire to own his own mine. He and his brother bought the Forest Queen a number of years back. While John finished his thirty years, his brother worked the mine. "Found some good ore," said John. "Up to twenty ounces a ton, down on the third level."

It was the two brothers who rigged up the cars, belts, and

weasel. I asked about the old steam tractor. "Got the old steam engine back in '46." John isn't much for words. You ask a question and you get a grin, and he hands you a map or a book to look it up — only occasionally resorting to speech.

I asked if he had done any mining before. "No — always wanted to — sort of a hobby."

"You don't go down these old shafts alone, do you?"

"Sure."

"Isn't that pretty dangerous?"

"Not smart enough to be scared," John replied.

Barry Davis, John's young friend, nodded agreement.

"Barry, I suppose you stay up topside to help out if John gets in trouble?"

"No, we go down together — we both get a kick out of it."

"You guys are nuts!"

"Yes."

Some of the old literature John pushed at me between cups of coffee contained glowing reports of a much younger Forest Queen Mine. At one time forty men were underground on each shaft. Pockets of wire silver were common. Five thousand dollars worth of silver was knocked down in a single blast.

The Chloride shaft at the foot of nearby Ruby Mountain was the object of some fancy promotion. In 1900, at the end of the silver boom, the English owner was awakened by the shaft boss and told of a rich pocket just uncovered. As the story goes, huge gobs of wire silver hung from the tunnel roof — and 3,500 pounds of nearly pure silver were pulled out. Later the straw boss bought the mine, then sold it at a profit by retelling the old story — slightly improved. The new owner failed to find any sign of silver, let alone "wire silver hanging in gobs."

A number of mines were promotional in nature, rather than productive. The Davy Crocket, Boomerang, Priceless, Last Chance, and Mountain Gem ran into isolated pockets of ore but none really paid off.

Bill Fisher found silver at the Forest Queen in 1879. The camp that grew up on the flats was originally called Ruby. The rush occurred in midwinter, and cabins had to be built quickly. Trees were cut down while deep snow lay on the ground. In the spring, numerous ten-foot stumps appeared.

Later, when the town grew, it was renamed after one of its founders, Dick Irwin. A promoter sold lots just south of

*John Hahn, retired artillery officer, is the present
owner of the Forest Queen Mine at Irwin.*

town at a second site called Ruby, promising five- and
six-story buildings. He skipped town, and the second Ruby
was swallowed up by Irwin.

At its peak in 1881, the population was close to 3,000. It
seemed to be a permanent town. Perhaps not a "helldorado" but, according to the newspaper, at least an "el-
dorado."

The editor of the town's paper, the *Elk Mountain Pilot*, was a strange character. He laid out the town cemetery, then became its first resident a few days later after he was killed dynamiting fish.

The town had three churches, seven sawmills, and a stamp mill. Lots sold for up to $5,000 each. Mines were subject to frequent sale. When it became evident that only a few shafts led to paying deposits, sales slacked, and the promoters left town. An elite social group called the Irwin Club, famous for entertaining two presidents, fell from a carefully selected membership of 100 in 1881 to a meager five in 1884. By 1909 the town was deserted.

John Hahn spends his winters in Boulder, Colorado. Otherwise, he is busy preparing to drill a tunnel into the mine from below. He figures to dewater the mine in that manner. Some of the best-paying ore is now under several hundred feet of water.

I inquired how he could tunnel into such a high-pressure spot without being drowned in the resulting deluge.

"Oh, that's not too difficult."

"I suppose you're going to get help to drive the tunnel?"

"No," he replied.

"That's pretty dangerous, isn't it?"

"Yes."

"Why do you keep doing it?"

"Well — it's a hobby — I like it." He paused, then added, "Don't you have any hobbies?"

"Yeah, I'm building a biplane in my garage."

John didn't say a damned thing — just sat there drinking coffee and grinning.

MAP NOTE: The townsite and nearby mines are at the juncture of the Mt. Axtell, Colorado, and the Oh-Be-Joyful, Colorado 7½ minute maps.

GOTHIC CITY, COLORADO

Truman Blacett found silver at the foot of Gothic Mountain in the fall of 1878. He grubbed out several hundred dollars worth of wire silver before vacating the high country for the winter.

Somehow his secret got out, and the next spring a hundred tents were pitched on the flats of East River near Blacett's claim. The area was 9,500 feet above sea level and still snow-covered. Tents pitched temporarily on snow had to be reset when the sun dried the ground.

Within four months, 170 "permanent" structures were up, and, as one wag put it, "the camp became visible to the naked eye."

Old pay shack in Gothic has been restored without benefit of paint.
Twelve-thousand-food Mt. Gothic is in background.

By the time Samuel Wail (Weil) marked out boundaries and applied for a town patent, the population had soared to 1,000. Within six months the settlement had grown to a sizable town with a butcher shop, hotel, two sawmills, and several stores. Indeed, the residents claimed it was not merely a town — it was GOTHIC CITY, the fastest growing piece of real estate in the world.

Within two years the town reached 8,000 population (according to the promoters) and may even have hit the 3,000 mark by accurate count. It now had two hotels, a town hall, two newspapers, and yet another newspaper editor was

Town Hall at Gothic was built in 1880 and has since been frequently braced, propped, and supported. Even the outside stairs are placed to counteract the lean.

Mountains to the north of Gothic are among Colorado's most beautiful. Aspen, world-famous ski area, is just over the top of Maroon and Pyramid peaks.

moving in a third press. There were two schools and a preacher in residence, busily attempting to neutralize the effects of two dance halls and half a dozen saloons.

Gothic City was one of the wildest towns in Colorado. Its red-light district was unequalled. Strangely enough, only one murder and one lynching were recorded during the four or five years that the city boomed.

In 1884 the veins thinned and the ore wouldn't pay expenses. Gothic City died almost as fast as it grew. The last election for mayor was between two newspaper editors. The winner, G. H. Judd, found himself mayor of a ghost town. He like it and assumed jurisdiction over all the ghost towns in the area. When he died, ashes of his cremated body were spread across the nearly barren flats of Gothic City.

The old town is called Gothic now — there is little excuse to add "city." The town hall and an old pay shack stand on the main street, braced with props and steel tie rods. Scattered about are a few of the original cabins. The Rocky Mountain Biological Laboratories have taken over the town as a summer teaching camp and research center. This science camp, like many of its kind, serves best as a vacation retreat for weary professors. Some of them are quite well known.

The summer climate in the area is delightful. The winters bring heavy snows ideal for skiing. A ski resort is presently undergoing rapid expansion at a point between Gothic and Crested Butte. It is booming much like Gothic City did 100 years ago.

MAP NOTE: The Mount Axtell and the O-Be-Joyful, Colorado, 7½ minute topographic maps are both required to study the area properly.

COLORADO AREA 3

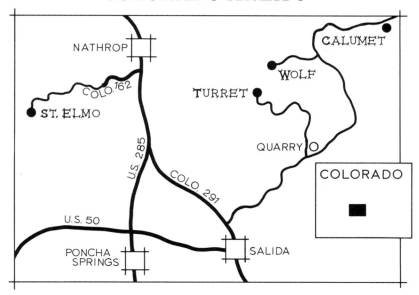

ST. ELMO, COLORADO

LIKE MOST MINES, the Mary Murphy was on an impossible site. You had to crawl to it, and if you weren't careful you could fall out of it. A mile-long tramway was built from the road on Chalk Creek, 1,700 feet up the slope, to the mine at a lofty elevation of 12,100 feet.

The small town of Romley sprouted at the lower end of the tramway. Three miles downstream, at a more liveable altitude, the town of Forest City was hacked out of the heavy timber. Most of the mine employees chose to live in the lower town.

In 1880 the townspeople of Forest City voted to incorporate. The postal department refused to accept the town's name, due to duplicate use in several other states in the Midwest and on the Pacific Coast. The townfolk settled on St. Elmo, after the title and hero of a best-selling novel by A. E. Wilson.

The town had 400 residents at the time but was destined to grow rapidly. By 1881 the population reached nearly two thousand. There was no shortage of wood, for the timber cleared from a homesite provided the sawlogs for the house.

The Denver and Rio Grande had cooperated with the

Union Pacific to run a rail line up Chalk Creek to St. Elmo, and work was in progress on an extension up the creek to Romley. The intent was to cross the continental divide via an 1,800-foot tunnel, then drop down to the town of Gunnison.

The tunnel was completed in 1882. The new line was hailed as a great achievement — until the first snow fell. Avalanches were so bad that the windows on the passenger coaches had to be boarded up. Snow and rocks frequently banged the sides of the cars. Some passengers appreciated the fact that they couldn't see out. On the downhill, eastern run through the tunnel, the train would pick up speed in order to blast through the heavy drift usually found just above Romley. Often the train would run under the drift and bog down. Trainmen would climb atop the observation car and run forward "shovel in hand"

St. Elmo, recently declared officially abandoned by the governor's office, has been a ghost town for many years.

The St. Elmo Fire Company and City Hall. Small, many-sided structure at front is a phone booth.

to open a smoke hole before the engineer and fireman suffocated. One summer day Mark Twain rode a flatcar down the grade, with one of the road bosses acting as brakeman. A bit of brake trouble added a new dimension to the outing. It was a wild ride, but the view through the "one big window" was unsurpassed.

St. Elmo quickly turned into a Saturday night hell-raising town. It had five hotels, a newspaper, numerous saloons, and no church. Eventually a school was built.

Church services were occasionally held there on Sundays. The Gunnison, Aspen, and Tin Cup Stage Lines ran daily trips from St. Elmo, up over Tin Cup Pass, and on down to the sister boomtown of Tin Cup.

Just below St. Elmo, less than a mile and across the creek, was the smelting town of Iron City. Never much for size, it became hard up for business when the railroad arrived. It lasted only two years. A flood on Chalk Creek furnished the coup de grace. Now it's a pretty nice spot to fish.

Obviously, the Miner's Exchange. Sign on door correctly indicates that fishing in the area is good.

*Sun and thin atmosphere of St. Elmo's high altitude
cause boards to bleach and curl rapidly.*

Only two of the fifty mines in the area were operating in
1897. The railroad ceased operation in 1911, and the tracks
were torn up in 1926. The town died that year, but the post
office hung on until 1952.

It's a beautiful ghost town now. Most of the buildings are
left, and there is no misplaced commercialism. One country

store operates much in the old style. It comes to life somewhat each winter when the snowmobilers gather on weekends to run the slopes above town. Occasionally a snowcat
races down the old railroad grade in pale imitation of Mark
Twain's thrilling ride.

MAP NOTE: St. Elmo is shown on the Garfield, Colorado, 15 minute
United States Geological Survey topographic map.

*Full moon highlights the fronts of buildings
along St. Elmo's main thoroughfare.*

TURRET, COLORADO

I'm lost without a map. Sometimes I'm lost with a map! A
trip into the upside-down country above Salida, Colorado,
was not in my plans, and my map file did not include the
Cameron Mountain topographic map. And in this case,
even with the map I would have been lost. At least the
towns of Calumet and Wolf, both near Turret, would always have been lost to me, since neither is shown on the
Cameron map.

With great good fortune I chanced to meet a gent named
Dave Smith. Dave operates a jeep tour service out of
Salida, Colorado. We were discussing items of mutual in-

*Ruins of the western portion of Turret viewed
from a rocky outcrop in center of town.*

terest — ghost towns — when Dave asked if I had ever heard of Turret. I hadn't, so he twisted the barb a little by adding, "How about Calument?"

"Nope."

"And Wolf? There's not a writer in the country ever even heard of that town!"

We left the next morning with a regular tour party. Lacking a map, I busily sketched the way in. In the process of sketching a map on six different pages of a notebook, I

City Hall overlooks central portion of Turret.

*Gregory Hotel has some of its interior walls papered
with old issues of the "Gold Belt."*

managed to botch the job properly. I didn't know where I was — but Dave did, and he was enjoying every mile of it.

Wolf and Calumet are to the right of the quarry and probably in Sections 21 and 24, respectively, on the aforementioned map. Turret is to the left of the quarry and on up a well-used road.

The road enters Turret at right angles to and in the middle of the town's deserted main street. To the left are the old post office and the former Turner residence, with the mine behind. A number of other buildings are nearby, some of which were saloons, others houses of ill fame, and still others combinations of the two.

Some distance to the right are the courthouse and main

business district of town. On the hill above and to the south
are the rock foundations of Turret's most popular speak-
easy, noted for its expansive underground moonshine
storage facilities.

The tin-covered hip roof of the courthouse gave protection to the mayor's office, sheriff's office, and jail. Just
down the slope the two-story log hotel, the Gregory,
sported walls papered with 1902 issues of the town's newspaper, the *Gold Belt*. Cat Gulch runs west through town,
parallel to the street. In places the boardwalk fronting the

*Henson's Mercantile and Meat Market, viewed
from porch of Gregory Hotel.*

stores was above the gulch and served as a bridge as well as a walkway.

In 1892 the town was actually three camps strung out along the gulch. At the high end was Adams Camp, then Minneapolis, then South Turret or Klondike. One historian states that the town was platted in 1897 under the name of Camp Austin. The place was officially named Turret in 1899, the year the town boomed. Population always varied with the seasons, with more than a thousand citizens in town during the summers of 1899 and 1900.

In 1900 the mines revealed the shallow nature of their

Log post office in foreground and Turner residence behind. Turner Mine tunnel entered the ground a few steps from the back door.

veins, and the town's future dimmed. Some gold and copper mining continued at the Independence Mine until 1916, but the best producers (the Golden Wonder, the Gold Bug, and the Monongahela) were worked out. The post office miraculously survived until 1941.

MAP NOTE: Turret is on the Cameron Mountain, Colorado, 15 minute United States Geological Survey topographic map.

Roofs of Turret catch the early morning light.

CALUMET, COLORADO
Much of the road from Salida to Calumet is coincident
with the grade of one of the most unusual rail lines ever
built in Colorado. The Denver and Rio Grande built the
spur to serve the Colorado Fuel and Iron Company. The
grade was set at seven percent, more than double the

*Trees now furnish the shade once offered by shingled porch
at rear entrance to Calumet's stage station.*

The stage station reached its full ninety-foot length when further construction was terminated by huge boulder.

normal slope. On the way up to the mines at Calumet, couplings on the train had a tendency to yield, resulting in wildly careening rides down the hill. To prevent such accidents, empty cars were pushed up; when filled, they were "held back" by the engine. Passengers were permitted to ride only after signing a release. From Calumet passengers could continue via the Turret, Whitehorn, and Salida Stage Line. The stage station for that line is one of the best remnants left in town. More than ninety feet long, it had a forge at one end and was built into and around a huge rock at the opposite northeast end. It is the longest log struc-

*Calumet's only residential building consists of four leaning
walls and drooping remnants of a covered porch.*

ture this observer has had the opportunity to photograph.
A second log building and an outhouse make up the balance of Calumet today. At one time it was a busy company
town, furnishing much of the iron ore for the smelters at
Pueblo, Colorado.

The Calumet Mine, for which the town was named, was
one of the deepest in the world prior to 1900. The shaft was
started in 1889 and in 1898 reached the end of the rich
magnetic iron ore deposits at a depth of 4,900 feet. Marble
found in the vicinity kept the town and the railroad in
business for a time, but for all practical purposes the life-
blood of Calumet flowed downhill with the last load of
magnetite.

MAP NOTE: Calumet is not shown on the Cameron Mountain, Colorado,
15 minute United States Geological Survey topographic map. A building
or two that might represent the town are shown in Section 24.

WOLF, COLORADO

No one seems to know the history of the town of Wolf, or, indeed, whether that is the correct name for the community. Dave Smith of Salida, Colorado, happened upon it some years ago while jeep-exploring in the area. He prowled about and found evidence of a main street and a dozen buildings, four or five of which still stand. The largest structure, a smelter, contains an old boiler, a forge, and worktables. On the wall is written:

A WOLF

Small smelter is the most impressive building in Wolf,
one of Colorado's least-known ghost towns.

Long unused, boiler in Wolf's smelter has become a prime nesting site for local birds.

Faint signs of intersecting streets can be made out. Trees nearly six inches in diameter grow in old ruts. Half a dozen cabins stand in varying states of decay.

An outhouse tilts on its foundation, threatening to fall into its own opening and self-destruct. Its seat is neatly carpeted — a substitute fur lining.

On one visit to the old town, Dave met a miner working on a claim. He was freshly returned from Alaska and was carrying out the required work to legally maintain his mine. He had scant information to offer concerning the town. He had heard that it boomed about 1898 and had a population of 200 at that time. When the boom eased seventy-five folk remained, mining and smelting the gold taken from shafts nearby. The miner did not know whether the town was called Wolf or Awolf — he'd heard it both ways.

Recently a rancher put cattle in the area. He provided water for the stock by digging in a number of old bathtubs. Except for the cattle tracks nearby, the sunken bathtubs would seem to add one more puzzle to the already mysterious town.

MAP NOTE: Wolf is not shown on the Cameron Mountain, Colorado, 15 minute United States Geological Survey topographic map; however, it is probably within the bounds of Section 21.

One of the finer homes in Wolf.

Trees grow in the middle of some homes in Wolf. Only faint traces of streets can be made out in this seldom-visited ghost town.

PART VI
UTAH

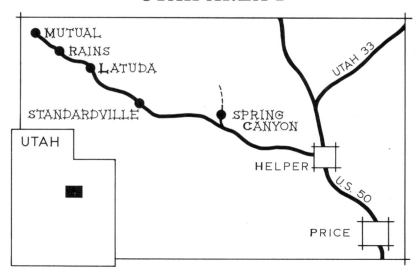

SPRING CANYON, UTAH

JESSE KNIGHT needed coal to operate the smelter he had just built in the Tintic mining district of Central Utah. The coal in Spring Canyon, west of the town of Helper, looked promising. Knight bought up 1,600 acres along the canyon and proceeded to build a town near the most accessible portion of the underground seam of coal.

He constructed sixty substantial sandstone homes along freshly graded streets. Next he built a number of frame company buildings, and finally he tapped the vein of coal. It can't be said that Knight lacked confidence. His judgment wasn't bad either, for more than eleven million tons of coal were eventually to be drawn from the mines above town.

Knight owned the mine, the town, and the buildings. He named the town "Storrs," after the man hired to supervise the operation. He would have named the town Knightsville, except that a community near his smelter already bore that name.

Before anyone moved into town, Knight laid down the rules. No gambling houses, no saloons, no red-light district, and no mercy for those who chose to be in violation. In spite of, or perhaps because of, the rules, the town quickly grew to a population of over 1,000, and production reached one hundred tons a day. During World War II production reached an all-time high of 2,000 tons per day. Population of the town, however, did not grow proportionately. Many citizens chose to live in nearby Helper.

During the postwar years production slacked, and the population dwindled. By 1959 only small crews worked the mine, and ten years later that minimal effort was terminated. The three families left in town moved out one by one. By 1972 the town was empty.

Flat spots are at a premium in the canyon. The town of Spring Canyon occupies the only sizable level area available. The school, bank, and hotel fill the narrow south end,

Spring Canyon (viewed from a hill north of town) shows clinic at right, company store in center, community showers at left.

*This solid rock structure, like many in Spring Canyon, was decapitated
to render it uninhabitable and therefore untaxable.*

while the company offices and store, along with the hospital, are squeezed into the equally narrow north end. The comparatively wide center section of town is filled with perhaps a dozen rows of residences, many still intact. Just north of town, half a mile or so, is a suburb consisting of small boardinghomes and a smattering of unique dugouts. Recesses in the sandstone canyon wall were deepened, and short walls were extended outward to form hybrid structures with truncated roofs.

As I poked about the deserted town I became aware of

other visitors. A young man, his wife, and two children were sightseeing. The father frequently stopped to point out buildings that seemed particularly meaningful to him. I approached him in hope of obtaining information concerning some buildings that I had found a bit puzzling.

Lewis Korenko, like most former residents of towns that have become deserted, greatly missed the opportunity to visit with old hometown friends. I was a poor second choice, but Lewis Korenko had so much conversation stored up he couldn't hold back.

Lewis, now a carpenter residing in Salt Lake City, moved with his folks to Spring Canyon in 1957, when the town was in its dying throes. His dad was a member of one of the last crews to work the mine. The crews were small, only four men working underground at a time. Maintenance work required as much effort as the actual mining of coal.

Rubble-strewn steps lead nowhere.

Company store in Spring Canyon sold general merchandise, including meat, groceries, clothing – even gasoline.

Water hydrants were boxed in to prevent freeze-up in cold weather.

Lone streetlight, long unlit, overlooks remains
of south end of Spring Canyon.

Lewis's father switched duty with a friend one day. That
day an explosion ripped through the mine. The four men
underground were killed. "Dad said it was the only time he
ever traded shifts," reported Lewis, "and he claimed he
would never do it again — felt real bad about it."

We wandered over toward the east edge of town. "Used
to be an overhead tram years ago — then they changed to
the track and cable cars," Lewis explained. "Whole thing
was gravity powered — loaded cars ran downhill all by
themselves." Lewis pointed to a small, flat spot high up
and across the big canyon. "Had a tennis court up there."
Before I could ask about chasing lost balls, Lewis proceeded to brief me on the town's suburbs. "Just around the
bend, up the canyon, was a bunch of homes — called the
place 'round the bend.'" Lewis pointed north. "Up Sow-

*Large machine shed is located in main canyon
at the south end of Spring Canyon.*

belly Canyon, before you get to the mine, those long buildings were boardinghouses run by Greeks, then later by the
Japanese."

We walked back to the main street of town and looked
over the old community bathhouse. Lewis asked if I planned to stay the night in town. "If you do, keep an eye out for
the White Lady. She wanders around the town wailing and
looking for her husband. He was killed down at Peerless
years ago. She's been seen by quite a few people running
the hills above town." Lewis waved to the west part of
town. "A young character, kind of looney himself, laid a
trap for the White Lady — put a bunch of explosives in a
house she was supposed to be haunting. Blew it up too!
He's in prison now, and the White Lady is still wailing
around town — he must not of got her."

Later, as the sun dropped below the canyon rim, I
watched the squirrels and chipmunks scurry about. Nooks
and crannies abound, and the rodents find no shortage of

housing or storage space. The inheritors of Spring Canyon lead a peaceful life. A life interrupted only by the occasional daytime visits of former residents, and the unpredictable nocturnal jaunts of the mysterious White Lady.

MAP NOTE: The 15 minute Castle Gate, Utah, United States Geological Survey topographic map, made in 1914, shows the town of Storrs, later renamed Spring Canyon.

Ad for Never-Rip overalls fills end of building in long-deserted town of Peerless, a few miles below the town of Spring Canyon.

STANDARDVILLE, UTAH

Mrs. Thelma Wilson, 75, of Helper, Utah, recalls much of interest concerning life in the town of Standardville. Her husband worked in the Standard Company Mines for twenty years. He worked six day weeks. Holidays were infrequent. Except for Christmas, the most memorable yearly celebration was Standard Day. Men got the day off, and the company provided entertainment and food. There were presents for all the kids under sixteen.

According to Thelma, Standardville came into existance about the same time as Spring Canyon. "There were still a number of people living in tents back in 1916 — but Standardville was growing fast. They had a big boarding-house for men, a church, company store, and of course there was a post office. There were dances at the commu-

Giant blower once sent life-giving air through the shafts and tunnels below Standardville.

nity hall, and we had a pitchur show. Always called it that
— pitchur show." Thelma rummaged through a box looking for old school photos. "Had school up to the ninth grade
for the children — sent them to Latuda for the tenth
grade."

The town had no jail or cemetery. Company towns,
Thelma explained, had little crime, and anyone who died

Seemingly rusted in position, like the Tin Man of "The Wizard
of Oz," this old crane stands immobile on the
outskirts of Standardville, Utah.

*Offices of the Standard Mining Company over-
look the remains of Standardville.*

was buried in Helper, just a few miles east at the mouth of
Spring Canyon.

The Miners' Museum in Helper contains an assortment
of old equipment, news clippings, and photographs. Many
of the photographs and mementos in the collection were
from the Standardville locality. Of particular note was the
pay voucher on display that showed one miner's tally for a
month's work:

4 hrs. labor @ 25¢	$ 1.00
110 cars — 224,370# coal @ 60¢ T.	60.11
Total Money Earned	$61.11
Charges:	
Hospital	$ 1.00
Coupons	30.11
Horses	30.00
	$61.11

At first glance it appears the miner just broke even. Actually, he had $30.11 in company money, either script or brass coins, with which to buy food, clothing, and lodging for the month. The charge for horses was explained by Fred Voll, caretaker of the museum. "Each man took a bunch of tags down the mine with him. When he got a car filled with ore, he hung his tag on the car, and it was hauled out by horses. The miner's tag was collected topside, his account credited for the coal, and a charge entered for the use of the horse." Unexplained was the fact that 224,370 pounds was a bit more than 112 tons and should have brought more than $61 in monies earned. Either the book-keeper or the miner was poor at figures.

There are no mines in Standardville today — just a few men working at salvaging the remains. The extensive metal coal tipples at the site are presently being disman-tled for scrap. Even the railroad rails are being cut by torch into loadable sections. Rusted equipment stands about: a crane, some loaders, and parts of an old caterpillar — all destined to be melted down.

On the hill northeast of town, the company office stands roofless, its cover sacrificed in the interest of lower taxes. Empty homes are scattered along otherwise empty streets.

It's pretty quiet in town now. Just the occasional snap and clang as cutting torches eat away at the remains — a far cry from Standard Day in Standardville.

MAP NOTE: The 15 minute Castle Gate, Utah, United States Geological Survey topographic map shows the town midway up Spring Canyon.

LATUDA, RAINS, AND MUTUAL, UTAH

The coal seam thickened at the upper end of Spring Canyon. A number of tunnels tapped the seam. Substantial towns mushroomed around three of the mines.

Latuda, established in 1914 as Liberty, grew to be the largest and the longest-lived of the three. It grew from twenty homes in 1918 to more than fifty-five in 1922. The town had to be renamed when a post office was established. There were too many towns already named Liberty. Latuda was chosen, in honor of the coal company responsible for the town's existence.

The town of Rains, less than a mile up the canyon from

Company offices of Latuda fill the narrow space between Main Street and bluff behind.

Old ore cars stand before the Rains Coal Company shops.

Welcome to the Mutual Store. Please watch your step.

*Latuda's small jail is still in working
order. Note the cast-in-place roof.*

Latuda, was established in 1915 by L. F. Rains, owner of
the Carbon Coal Company. The Rains Mine was one of the
biggest producers in the canyon, reaching 2,000 tons per
day at its peak. The town grew on either side of the single
road along the canyon floor. As the population increased,
new houses were built up the canyon, close to the outskirts
of another town springing up around the Mutual Mine.

Mutual, established in 1921, never grew larger than 250
residents. Its mine, on the thickest part of the seam, had
great potential, but production during its best year never
equalled the amount brought out of the Rains Mine in a
two-week period. When the Mutual Mine shut down in
1938, residents of a tent town by the Little Standard Mine,
half a mile away, moved into the vacant houses. The company store was bought out by one of the new citizens and
continued in business until 1954, when Mutual, the up-
permost town, became deserted. The towns down the
canyon closed in sequence.

The Rains Mine closed down in 1958. The Latuda Coal
Company continued to operate until 1966. Houses from the

*Tall coal tipple stands in rigid support of platform matching
level of tunnel penetrating hill behind.*

*Cattle wander through remains of old gas
station at north end of Mutual.*

*Long-unused shop of small unnamed coal mine above Mutual
offers scenic view of the head of Spring Canyon.*

three towns were sold off and hauled down the canyon to Helper and Price.

The old company building still marks the center of Latuda. Just east, the little stone jail stands in useable condition. Below the jail are a number of dugout garages.

Up the canyon a short distance, at the site of Rains, two of the original, wooden coal cars stand at the side of the road. Behind are the machine shops of the Carbon Coal Company.

At Mutual most of the mine complex is in place. The old store still has its sign over the side door. Farther up the canyon are numerous frame houses in various states of destruction. Cattle roam freely about, around, and occasionally through, the old homes.

There is little sign of the activity that once filled the canyon. The coal is gone now — all thirty million tons of it.

MAP NOTE: The Castlegate, Utah, 15 minute United States Geological Survey topographic map fails to show any of these towns. They are easily located, however, by driving up the main canyon from Standardville.

UTAH AREA 2

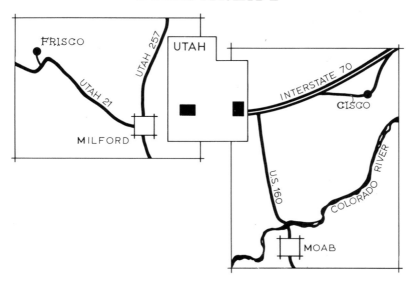

FRISCO, UTAH

FRISCO AND CISCO, two of Utah's most unusual ghost towns, are a study in contrasts. Frisco, at the western edge of the state, was a mining town. Cisco, a state's width to the east, was a railroading community. Both were born in the mid-1870s. Frisco was wild and short-lived. Cisco was mild and more durable. Frisco has been a ghost for almost one hundred years. Cisco, Utah's newest ghost town, met its demise in 1970, a victim of progress.

To most observers ghost towns are like antiques — valuable only when aged. The true aficionado might disagree. Some items are worthy of preservation from the moment of disuse. A particular buggy whip with a long and faithful history is deserving of a spot on the mantle the same day the horse is traded in on the Model T.

Some ghost towns are worthy of veneration the day they die. Johnny Cash felt that way about Cisco even before the town had completely expired. But first, the history of Frisco, and then Cisco — the contrast is enhanced if the story travels with the flow of time.

Jim Ryan and Sam Hawkes, veteran prospectors, left Pioche, Nevada, in the summer of '75. They headed east, skirting the southern slopes of the Needle Range, then headed north into the heart of the San Francisco Mountains.

At Squaw Springs the two prospectors decided to give their pack animals a few days' graze on the comparatively lush grass that grew about the water hole. They prospected the area leisurely, with little success. Returning from one last look at a nearby blowout, one of the prospectors took a passing whack at a small, light-colored outcrop. The limestone cleaved to reveal a heavy streak of shiny grey silver.

*Machine shop in center catered to repair work
for numerous mines in the Frisco area.*

*One of several great holes in the mountain, as seen from
company offices in mining area just west of Frisco.*

Ryan and Hawkes made permanent camp immediately,
then proceeded to blast a hole in pursuit of the precious
metal. The vein thickened, and at twenty-five feet below
the surface it looked like a salable prospect. When offered
$25,000 for their mine, Ryan and Hawkes were quick to
take the money, retire from mining, and get back to prospecting.

Twin skips of the Horn Silver (or King David)
Mine had rock deflectors overhead.

The new owners pushed the shaft (now called the Horn
Silver) to a depth of nearly 300 feet. The vein held, and
nearly $2 million worth of ore was removed.

Figuring the deposit was near depletion, owners of the
Horn Silver let out word that the mine was for sale. Jay
Cooke, once an influential financier, now broke and pur-
sued by creditors, bought the mine with the scavenged

remains of his fortune. The purchase price of $5 million was met by a little cash, some loans, and a lot of promises. Cooke intended to go for broke. Neither Cooke nor the sellers were aware that the Horn Silver was yet to reach its prime. It would eventually produce more than $20 million in silver for its owners.

Settlements were scattered about the area — some near the mine, others strung out along the foot of the mountain. When the Utah Southern Railroad extended its tracks

Waste dump overlooks flats once occupied by the west suburb of Frisco.

another 200 miles to the Horn Silver, population in the area took a sudden leap. The various communities amalgamated, and a town grew beside the tracks one mile east of the mine.

The town took its name from 9,725-foot San Francisco Peak, just a few miles to the north, but already that name had been shortened to Frisco Peak. Knowing full well that the town would be called Frisco, the citizens chose to make the short version official. In time the peak was renamed Frisco to match the town.

By 1880 Frisco had reached its zenith in size and temperament. Twenty-three saloons offered vice in the fullest spectrum. Tenderloin ladies solicited on the main floor and

Small dugout residence had fancy raised kitchen behind front room.

Inside of fancy dugout shows ceiling and walls in need of repair.

utilized the rooms above on a rotating basis. Whiskey was bad, and the gambling tables crooked.

Living was expensive, but life was cheap. The lives of many miners had already been shortened by the high temperatures and bad dust in the mine. Most of them suffered from some degree of miners' consumption.

Under these conditions tempers flared quickly and fights were common. Some claim that Frisco would have been a sizable town if so many citizens hadn't killed each other. The local mortician toured the back alleys each morning, picking up bodies, and burying them for whatever he could rifle from their clothing.

A few upright citizens determined that the situation was out of hand. A reformed gunslinger by the name of Pearson was hired to bring respectability to Frisco. Pearson's idea of law and order was to declare open season on anyone he figured was undesirable. He offered the offenders a choice

— get out of town or draw. Often the hard cases chose the latter and, as often, lost. Pearson was fast. His opponents invariably died of a bad case of "slow." One reporter claimed he dispatched six men in one day. Within six weeks the town was respectable — if somewhat smaller.

In 1885, after ten years of continuous operation, disaster struck the Horn Silver. Luckily there was no loss of life. The men coming off shift had just left the skip and the new shift was about to do down, when a trembling was felt in the gallows frame and cable. The tremble repeated, then a low rumble was heard as 900 feet of vertical shaft caved in.

Observers claimed the cave-in caused a shock wave of such proportion that windows were broken in Milford, fifteen miles away. It would be far more logical to assume that an earth tremor was the cause of both the cave-in and the damage in Milford.

Miners were laid off as small crews set to work drilling the 900 feet of newly filled shaft. The smelters closed down for lack of work. In turn, operators of the charcoal ovens went broke, and woodcutters found no market for their product.

Frisco was wiped out overnight. Even when the mine resumed operations, Frisco remained largely deserted. Mining crews stayed at the mine or commuted from Milford.

There is little to be seen at the town site — a few foundations and remnants of one store. But the Horn Silver, a mile to the west, is still reasonably intact.

Hoisting cables are in place, holding double-barrelled skips at surface level. Gallows wheels atop the hoist are of unique design. They are flat-bottomed and deep-rimmed to hold the old-fashioned flat "ribbon cable" of the type used in Bodie, California. Centered in the flat surface of the gallows wheel is a semicircular depression to guide the more modern round cable. Round cable is now on the drums of the hoist. No sign of the old flat cable could be found.

Down the hill a bit, just in front of a massive excavation in the rocky hillside, stand half a dozen mine buildings and the foundations of the two smelters. To the side a number of low log and rock soddies fight a losing battle with the elements. Up the ravine a freshening breeze loosens another rusted sheet of corrugated metal on the old hoist house.

It is interesting to speculate on how the course of history

Sunset over the King David.

might have changed if Ryan or Hawkes had not succumbed to the urge to give that small outcrop of limestone a passing whack.

MAP NOTE: The Frisco, Utah, 15 minute United States Geological Survey topographical map shows the town, the Horn Silver Mine, and a number of additional mines in the area.

CISCO, UTAH

Cisco, after nearly eighty-five years of serving the travelers' needs, became a ghost when the interstate highway bypassed the arteries of town. One general store remained open in the vain hope that enough people would remain in town to keep it in business. The owner wanted to raise his family and live out his life in the small country town he had come to love. It soon became obvious that his hopes would not be realized; he would inevitably have to uproot his family and begin a new life.

That's when Johnny Cash happened through town. Intrigued by the unusual situation, he remained in town throughout the day and into the evening. One of the few residents in town at the time reported that he spent $7.11 — more than anyone had spent in months. Johnny bought a round of beer or two as he listened to stories about Cisco. He was particularly taken by the pathos of the father who must take his family to a new town — whose kids could never come back to visit old friends — whose kids would not have a meaningful hometown, until time and new experience could provide new memories.

Johnny wrote a song about Cisco. He drew on its early history for the title, "Cisco Clifton Station." It isn't one of Johnny Cash's better songs, but it was the most popular tune on the juke box at the old store in Cisco.

The finite history of Cisco began in the mid-1880s. John Martin, surveyor for the narrow-gage railroad, laid out the section of the line connecting Mack, Colorado, with Thompson, Utah. The area between the Book Cliffs and the Colorado River was of particular interest to him. He chose to settle on land adjacent to the tracks. In 1887 he applied for and was granted a post office for the settlement that grew about his original homestead.

A second community was growing two miles away, centered about a restaurant and store. Victor Hanson, owner of the store, may have had some inside information, since the new wide-track rail lines were shortly to run past his holdings.

John Martin's settlement folded, and Hanson's town, now laid out with a full set of streets, was granted its own post office under the name of Cisco.

The name given Martin's original post office became

Hotel, motel, and cafe, the last business to close in Cisco.

clouded with the move. Some folks say it was Martinsdale, others Book Cliffs, or Clifton Station.

Soon new stores were springing up in Cisco, between main street and the railroad tracks. Boxcar-loads of ice were hauled in to preserve produce and cool the palate. The tourist trade via railroad and horse-drawn wagon gave the town sustenance and reason for growth. Later the highway through town was surfaced, and Cisco's future seemed assured.

Early in the present century gold and silver were found in the La Sal Mountains a few miles south. Oil was considered likely in the area near town, and numerous rigs moved in to tap the faults and domes that hopefully existed in the strata deep beneath the surface.

The first barrel of crude was pumped from the Cisco Well on February 6, 1904. The Cisco Mercantile paid the owners $100, and the town celebrated. The newly finished hotel was booked solid. Later additional wells brought in abun-

The Cisco Motel advertised "every room individually heated."

Open 24 hours.

dant supplies of natural gas. The Cisco Gas Wells were the
biggest producers in Utah during the late twenties.

Cisco had oil and gas, but local water was scarce. The
scarcity seemed of little note as long as the railroad kept
pumping water from the Colorado River to the standpipe
in town. For sixty years the railroad and town folk shared
the cost, to their mutual benefit. When the railroad retired
its steam engines, it no longer had need of large quantities
of water. The pumps were shut down, and Cisco's water
supply dried up.

It took twelve days for town representatives to obtain a
judgment. The railroad was told to continue its part of the
bargain, whether it need water for its diesels or not.

In the late sixties, word leaked out that major highway
improvement was being considered. Highway 50 passing
through town was to be made part of the new four-lane
interstate network. Owners of gas stations and motels
made plans to enlarge and update their establishments.
Then the bad news arrived: The new highway was to take a
short cut across the bend that Cisco occupied. Access to
town would be a dozen miles away in either direction.

Residents rushed to sell their homes and businesses before the word could spread. Potential buyers were made
wary by the proliferation of "For Sale" signs all about
town.

Cisco had contracted a terminal illness. As work started
on the interstate it became obvious that the town had only
a year or so to live. The six gas stations closed down like
dominoes in a line. Stores and motels closed, until only one
remained open, the one in which Johnny Cash spent $7.11.

That was several years ago, and now that store is deserted. The juke box is still inside, full of records, but there
is no one around to play "Cisco Clifton Station."

MAP NOTE: Cisco is shown in detail on the Cisco, Utah, 15 minute United
States Geological Survey topographic map. The location of the town is
also shown on most highway maps.

Old drilling rig stands like a monument over deserted Cisco.

BIBLIOGRAPHY

Bancroft, Caroline. *Six Racy Madams*. Boulder, Colo.: Johnson Publishing Co., 1965.

Barnes, Will C. *Arizona Place Names*. Univ. of Arizona General Bulletin No. 2. Tucson, Ariz.: Univ. of Arizona Press, 1935.

Beebe: Lucius M., and Clegg, C. M. *The American West: The Pictorial Epic of a Continent*. New York: E. P. Dutton and Co., Inc., 1955.

Brown, Robert L. *An Empire of Silver*. Caldwell, Idaho: The Caxton Printers, Ltd., 1965.

———. *Ghost Towns of the Colorado Rockies*. Caldwell, Idaho: The Caxton Printers, Ltd., 1971.

———. *Jeep Trails to Colorado Ghost Towns*. Caldwell, Idaho: The Caxton Printers, Ltd., 1963.

———. *Colorado Ghost Towns, Past and Present*. Caldwell, Idaho: The Caxton Printers, Ltd., 1972.

Buffum, E. Gould. *Six Months in the Gold Mines*. Los Angeles: The Ward Ritchie Press, 1958.

California State Parks and Recreational Department. *California Historical Landmarks*. Sacramento: 1968.

Carr, Stephen L. *The Historical Guide to Utah Ghost Towns*. Salt Lake City, Utah: Western Epics Publishing Co., 1972.

Caughey, John W. *Gold is the Cornerstone*. Berkeley: Univ. of California Press, 1948.

Colorado Magazine. July, 1940; March, 1941; July, 1941; January, 1942.

Cook, Fred S. *Legends of the Southern Mines*. California Traveler, no date.

Daughters of the Utah Pioneers. *Grand Memories*. Grand County, Utah: 1972.

Driggs, Howard R. *Westward America*. New York: G. P. Putnam's Sons, 1942.

Eberhart, Perry. *Guide to the Colorado Ghost Towns and Mining Camps*. Denver, Colo.: Sage Books, 1959.

Fisher, Vardis, and Holmes, Opal Laurel. *Gold Rushes and Mining Camps of the Early American West*. Caldwell, Idaho: The Caxton Printers, Ltd., 1968.

Florin Lambert. *Western Ghost Towns*. Seattle, Wash.: Superior Publishing Co., 1961.

———. *Ghost Town Trails*. Seattle, Wash.: Superior Publishing Co., 1964.

———. *Ghost Town Treasures*. Seattle, Wash.: Superior Publishing Co., 1965.

Gude, Erwin G. *California Place Names*. Berkeley: Univ. of California Press, 1969.

Hall, Frank. *History of the State of Colorado*. Chicago: Chicago Blakely Printing Co., 1889.

Hill, Rita. *Then and Now, Here and There Around Shakespeare*. Lordsburg, N. Mex.: Privately printed, 1963.

Huber, Joe. *The Story of Madrid*. Albuquerque: Privately printed, 1963.

Jackson, Joseph Henry. *Anybody's Gold: The Story of California's Mining Towns*. San Francisco: Chroncile Books, 1970.

Jackson, Joseph Henry, ed. *Gold Rush Album*. New York: Charles Scribner's Sons, 1949.

Jackson, William Henry. *Picture Maker of the Old West*, with text based on diaries and notebooks. Edited by Clarence S. Jackson. New York: Charles Scribner's Sons, 1947.

Johnson, Robert Niel. *Southwestern Ghost Town Atlas*. Susanville, Calif.: Cy Johnson and Son, 1973.

Lee, Bourke. *Death Valley, The Immortal Desert*. New York: Random House, Inc., 1974.

Lockwood, Frank C. *Pioneer Days in Arizona*. New York: The Macmillan Co., 1932.

Looney, Ralph. *Haunted Highways*. New York: Hastings House, 1968.

McDowell, Jack, Editor. *Ghost Towns of the West*. Menlo Park, Calif.: Lane Magazine & Book Co., 1971.

Miller, Joseph. *Arizona: The Last Frontier*. New York: Hastings House, 1956.

Murbarger, Nell. *Ghosts of the Glory Trail*. Palm Desert, Calif.: Desert Printers, Inc., 1956.

Myrick, David F. *Railroads of Nevada and Eastern California*. Berkeley: Howell-North Books, 1962.

Nadeau, Remi. *Ghost Towns and Mining Camps of California*. Los Angeles: The Ward Ritchie Press, 1965.

Paher, Stanley W. *Nevada Ghost Towns and Mining Camps*. Berkeley: Howell-North Books, 1970.

Reeve, Frank D. *History of New Mexico*. New York: Lewis Historical Publishing Co., 1961.

Rolle, Andrew F. *California: A History*. New York: Thomas Y. Crowell Co., 1969.

Sherman, James E. and Barbara H. *Ghost Towns of Arizona*. Norman, Okla.; Univ. of Oklahoma Press, 1969.

Silverberg, Robert. *Ghost Towns of the American West*. New York: Thomas Y. Crowell Co., 1968.

Stong, Phil. *Gold In Them Hills*. Garden City, N.Y.: Doubleday & Co., Inc., 1957.

United States Forest Service. Maps of the National Forests of the Southwestern States.

United States Geological Survey. Topographic maps of areas of interest in the Southwestern States.

Utah Historical Quarterly. Selected issues, 1928-33.

Wagner, Jack R. *Gold Mines of California*. Berkeley: Howell-North Books, 1970.

Watkins, T. H. *Gold and Silver in the West.* Palo Alto, Calif.: American West Publishing Co., 1971.

Wolle, Muriel Sibell. *The Bonanza Trail.* Bloomington: Indiana Univ. Press, 1958.

Woods, Betty. *Ghost Towns and How to Know Them.* Santa Fe, N. Mex.: Press of the Territorian, 1969.

Young, Otis E. Jr., *Western Mining.* Norman, Okla.: Univ. of Oklahoma Press, 1970.

INDEX